Comfort for Troubled Hearts

Comfort for Troubled Hearts

by
John MacArthur, Jr.

WORD OF GRACE COMMUNICATIONS
P.O. Box 4000
Panorama City, CA 91412

© 1986 by
JOHN F. MACARTHUR, JR.

All Scripture quotations, unless noted otherwise, are from the *New Scofield Reference Bible*, King James Version. Copyright © 1967 by Oxford University Press, Inc. Reprinted by permission.

Library of Congress Cataloging in Publication Data

MacArthur, John F.
    Comfort for troubled hearts.

    (John MacArthur's Bible studies)
    Includes index.
    1. Bible. N.T.   John XIV, 1-14—Criticism, interpretation, etc. 2. Bible. N.T. John XVI, 16 33—Criticism, interpretation, etc. I. Title. II. Series: MacArthur, John F. Bible studies.
BS2615.2.M277   1986   226'.506   86-21753
ISBN 0-8024-5342-2 (pbk.)

1 2 3 4 5 6 Printing / GB / Year 91 90 89 88 87 86

Printed in the United States of America

Contents

These Bible studies are taken from messages delivered by Pastor-Teacher John MacArthur, Jr., at Grace Community Church in Panorama City, California. These messages have been combined into a 6-tape album entitled *Comfort for Troubled Hearts*. You may purchase this series either in an attractive vinyl cassette album or as individual cassettes. To purchase these tapes, request the album *Comfort for Troubled Hearts* or ask for the tapes by their individual GC numbers. Please consult the current price list; then, send your order, making your check payable to:

WORD OF GRACE COMMUNICATIONS
P.O. Box 4000
Panorama City, CA 91412

Or call the following number:
818-982-7000

1

Who Goes When Jesus Comes?

Outline

Introduction
A. The Consolation to the Disciples
B. The Consternation of the Disciples
C. The Concern for the Disciples

Lesson
  I. Trust in Christ's Presence (v. 1)
     A. The Confusion of the Disciples
        1. The anticipation
        2. The anxiety
     B. The Comfort from the Lord
        1. The comfort explained
        2. The comfort examined
     C. The Connection with the Holy Spirit
 II. Trust in Christ's Promises (vv. 2-3)
     A. The Preparation of Heaven (v. 2)
        1. The location of our future home
        2. The layout of our future home
        3. The life-style in our future home
        4. The looks of our future home
     B. The Plan to Receive Us (v. 3)
        1. The Lord's promise
        2. The Lord's desire
III. Trust in Christ's Person (vv. 4-6)
     A. The Inquiry
     B. The Instruction
     C. The Insurance

Introduction

John 14:1-6 says, "Let not your heart be troubled; ye believe in God, believe also in me. In my Father's house are many mansions; if it were not so, I would have told you. I go to prepare a place for you. And if I go and prepare a place for you, I will come again, and receive you unto myself, that where I am, there ye may be also. And where I go ye know, and the way ye know. Thomas saith unto him, Lord, we know not where thou goest; and how can we know the way? Jesus saith unto him, I am the way, the truth, and the life; no man cometh unto the Father, but by me."

Those six verses constitute one of the most familiar texts in all the Bible. Many people learn it as children in Sunday school. I did, and it has always been one of my favorite passages. The central thought in it is Christ's returning to receive us.

A. The Consolation to the Disciples

Every Christian knows that Jesus is coming back. We have always talked about that, but there seems to be a new anticipation in our day. Jesus could come in this generation because there aren't many more prophecies that have to be fulfilled before He returns. Everything is becoming ready. However, our hope in Jesus Christ is not restricted to awaiting His return. Some people say, "Yes, Jesus is coming back, but can He comfort us now in times of deep tragedy and severe pain?" John 14 answers that question. The whole chapter tells of Christ's promise to give us comfort. Not only can we anticipate His return, but we can also know He will provide comfort for us in the present. You could call John 14 "the comfort chapter." It details Christ's promise of His future return and the present comfort He offers to His disciples. He said He would send them the Comforter, the Holy Spirit.

B. The Consternation of the Disciples

The scene of that passage is the upper room, where the disciples gathered with Jesus the night before He went to Golgotha to die on the cross. Judas had already been dismissed to carry out his betrayal (John 13:27). Jesus had begun His last address to the remaining eleven disciples. In a short while, their world was going to collapse into unbelievable chaos. In chapter 14, they are beginning to experience pain and hurt. They are bewildered and worried in response to the news that their beloved Master, whom they had been willing to die for, was leaving them. In John 11, when Jesus says He is going to Jerusalem, Thomas says, "Let us also go, that we may die with him" (v. 16).

The disciples' hearts were torn when Christ told them He was going away. You may know what it's like to be permanently separated from someone you deeply love. You can imagine the excruciating pain the disciples felt at the news that they would lose the One who loved them with a perfect love. Jesus anticipated their anxiety and in John 14 gives them comfort upon comfort. That's why John 14 can be called "the comfort chapter." In fact, Martin Luther called it "the best and most comforting sermon preached by Christ while on this earth . . . a jewel and a treasure not purchasable with the world's goods" (*Sermons on the Gospel of St. John* from the series *Luther's Works*, vol. 24 [St. Louis: Concordia, 1961], p. 7).

C. The Concern for the Disciples

As we study John 14:1-6, you'll see that those verses not only discuss comfort but also reveal Christ in all His glory. You can't help but recognize the uniqueness of Jesus. Any other man who knew he would have to die on a cross, bear the sins of every person who ever lived, be forsaken by the Father, and be persecuted would have been so preoccupied with his circumstances that he wouldn't have been able to focus on anyone else's needs. But Jesus did. Even though He knew about the horrible things that would soon happen to Him, He was completely absorbed with the needs of His eleven disciples. He wanted to prepare them for the shock they would experience. Jesus felt the weight of the sin He would bear and knew He was about to taste the bitter cup of death for every man. But He still took a primary interest in the sorrow and fears of His disciples.

Christ's concern for the disciples reminds me of John 13:1: "He loved them unto the end." And as you study John 14:1-6, you will recognize that passage as the foundation for comfort not only for the disciples but for us as well. If you find you are always anxious and unable to find rest, you'll find John 14:1-6 to be a soothing Scripture passage.

The basis of comfort comes from trusting the Lord. If you are discontent, anxious, or worried, it's because you don't trust Christ. In John 14:1-6, Jesus tries to comfort the disciples by saying in effect, "I want you to trust these three things: My presence, My promises, and My Person." If you really trust Christ, you won't worry. The reason the disciples became anxious when the Lord said He would leave was that they were focusing on their problems instead of trusting Christ. So He told them to trust Him.

Lesson

I. TRUST IN CHRIST'S PRESENCE (v. 1)

Jesus told the disciples in John 14:1, "Let not your heart be troubled; ye believe in God, believe also in me."

A. The Confusion of the Disciples

1. The anticipation

Let's look first at the statement "Let not your heart be troubled." According to the Greek text, Christ wasn't saying, "Don't let your hearts start becoming troubled"; He was saying, "Stop letting your hearts be troubled." The disciples were already perplexed and filled with a medley of emotions. To them, everything seemed to be falling apart. Their dreams and desires were unraveling. The gloomy prospect of Christ's dying and leaving them was terrifying. They were convinced He was the Messiah, but they had envisioned Him as an illustrious conqueror. Their hopes had risen high when Jesus went riding into Jerusalem as everyone placed palm branches in His path and cried, "Hosanna to the Son of David!" (Matt. 21:8-9). But just when their excitement was at fever pitch, Christ began to talk about His death. He said, "Except a grain of wheat fall into the ground and die, it abideth alone; but if it die, it bringeth forth much fruit" (John 12:24). That filled the disciples with sorrow because they really loved Jesus. The thought of losing Him was unbearable. How could they reconcile His death

10

with His messiahship? What kind of a way was that to treat them? They had forsaken all to follow Him, and now He was going to leave them in the midst of enemies who hated Him and them.

2. The anxiety

In addition to all that, the disciples had failed to show their love for Jesus in John 13. While in the upper room, they were so filled with pride and selfishness that they didn't wash one another's feet. It wasn't until Jesus finally did the task Himself that they recognized their self-centeredness. They were also perplexed because Jesus said one of them would betray Him (John 13:21). They didn't know who it was, even when Jesus dismissed Judas. They thought Judas had gone out to buy bread or do an errand. To make things worse, they heard Jesus tell Peter, who appeared to be the strongest disciple of all, that he would deny Him three times (John 13:38). Everything seemed to be coming to a disappointing climax. They must have been thinking, "What is going on here?" Yet they still had an undying love for the Lord.

B. The Comfort from the Lord

Jesus could read the disciples' hearts. He knew exactly what they were thinking. He was able to feel their infirmities and sorrows. They couldn't feel His pain, but He could feel theirs. There is always room in His heart for the troubles of others. He feels people's griefs as if they were His own. So in John 14, He kindly comforts them. He does that even though He knows they will soon forsake Him. Isaiah said of Jesus, "In all their affliction he was afflicted" (Isa. 63:9). He also said that Christ was anointed "to bind up the brokenhearted" (61:1). He was given "the tongue of the learned, that [He] should know how to speak a word in season to him who is weary" (50:4). Christ was able to feel the pain of the disciples and comfort them. He was the agonized Shepherd facing the cross, yet He comforted the sheep who were going to be scattered. In the hymn "Souls of Men, Why Will Ye Scatter?" nineteenth-century hymn writer William Bradbury said, "Was there ever kinder shepherd, half so gentle, half so sweet?"

1. The comfort explained

At the end of John 14:1 Jesus says, "Ye believe in God, believe also in me." Christ was telling the disciples to trust in His presence. In that statement, He made Himself equal with God. Now that could be an imperative or an indicative in the Greek. He could have commanded them to believe in God and believe in Him. Or He could have said factually, "You believe in God; you believe in Me." But the best translation seems to be, "You believe in God (fact); believe also in Me (command)." That puts Him on an equal plane with God. Jesus commanded His disciples to continue to trust Him even though they wouldn't be able to see Him. They believed in God even when they couldn't see Him, and Jesus wanted them to believe in Him in the same way.

2. The comfort examined

King David said, "I had fainted, unless I had believed to see the goodness of the Lord in the land of the living" (Ps. 27:13). In another psalm we read, "Mine eyes are unto thee, O God, the Lord; in thee is my trust" (Ps. 141:8). The Israelites, including the Pharisees, believed in God. Christ wanted the disciples to believe in Him as they did in God. In their darkest hour, He told them to trust Him. Just because they wouldn't be able to see Him didn't mean He wouldn't be present.

The kind of belief Jesus talks about in John 14:1 isn't the same as the belief expressed in salvation. He wasn't saying, "Believe in Me and you'll be saved." The disciples were already saved. The word translated "believe" in John 14:1 is in the present tense in the Greek text, which conveys the concept of continual trust. Jesus asked the twelve to keep on trusting Him even though He wouldn't be visible to them anymore.

The apostles had already recognized Jesus as the Son of God by divine illumination. But their faith was like Thomas's. After the resurrection, Thomas was told Christ was alive, but he doubted the news. He said he wouldn't believe until he saw Christ and put his hand in the nail prints (John 20:25). That's the basis upon which Jesus appeared to Thomas (John 20:27-29). But when your faith is based on sight, you're operating on the lowest level of faith. Up to now, the disciples had seen Jesus and all that He had done. Soon He would leave them and become invisible to the physical eye. So He in effect told them, "My leaving you shouldn't be a problem. You believe in God even though you don't see Him."

In Deuteronomy 31:6, Moses tells the people of Israel, "Be strong and of good courage, fear not, nor be afraid . . . for the Lord thy God, he it is who doth go with thee; he will not fail thee, nor forsake thee." The Jewish people firmly believed that God was with them. Jesus reminded the disciples of that fact. They believed in God even though they had never seen His form. They trusted in His care without ever seeing a protecting hand. They had full faith in an invisible God! And Jesus wanted them to continue believing in Him when He was no longer visible.

In John 20:29, after Christ shows Thomas His nail prints, He says, "Thomas, because thou hast seen me, thou hast believed; blessed are they that have not seen, and yet have believed." In Matthew 28:20 He says, "Lo, I am with you always." He will never leave us or forsake us (Heb. 13:5). That's the same promise God gives in Deuteronomy 31:6.

C. The Connection with the Holy Spirit

Jesus promised He would send the Holy Spirit to the disciples. They could have thought Christ was leaving them for good. But notice what the Holy Spirit was to do. Christ said, "When he, the Spirit of truth, is come, he will guide you into all truth; for he shall not speak of himself, but whatever he shall hear, that shall he speak; and he will show you things to come. He shall glorify me; for he shall receive of mine, and shall show it unto you" (John 16:13-14).

The Holy Spirit's ministry is to keep reminding us of Christ's presence. He is the guarantee that Christ exists. In John 16:15 Christ says, "All things that the Father hath are mine; therefore said I, that he shall take of mine, and shall

13

show it unto you." The Spirit's ministry is to show us Christ. So when Jesus told the disciples to believe in Him just as they believed in the invisible God, He said He would send the Holy Spirit, who would remind them of His presence. The Spirit's ministry is to point to Christ. That's why any ministry that centers on the Holy Spirit is dangerous, because Christ doesn't get the glory.

The first way Jesus comforted the disciples was by assuring them of His presence. I have never seen Jesus Christ, but there is no one in existence whom I believe in more than He. He is alive and real. I know Him; I talk to Him. I sense His presence. No one will ever convince me He's not alive. The Spirit of God witnesses to me continually that Christ lives. Although I can't see Him, I trust Him.

Where Is Christ?

Jesus wanted the disciples to trust Him even though they couldn't see Him. He said, "Ye believe in God, believe also in me" (John 14:1). The word *also* in John 14:1 is important. It shows the equality between Christ and God. So whatever situation you are in or whatever problem you face, just remember: the Lord is present. You might think it would be nice if He were visible, but then He wouldn't be able to be everywhere He is needed. When Christ was a person in the New Testament era, He was able to be in only one place at a time. But now His presence is revealed by the Holy Spirit to all believers at the same time. We may not see Him, but He's there.

II. TRUST IN CHRIST'S PROMISES (vv. 2-3)

A. The Preparation of Heaven (v. 2)

Our Lord says in John 14:2, "In my Father's house are many mansions; if it were not so, I would have told you. I go to prepare a place for you." You can imagine how thrilled the disciples were to hear that Christ was going to the Father to prepare a place for them. That promise gave them a whole new perspective. Christ wasn't going away to leave them; He was going away to get heaven ready for them. What a thought! Jesus said He was going to His Father's house. I love the way He addressed God as *Father*.

Jesus, who had dwelt eternally in the bosom of the Father, came forth to reveal the Father. Now that His work would soon be done, He was planning to return to full glory with the Father.

1. The location of our future home

What was Christ talking about when He referred to His Father's house? He was speaking about heaven. In the New Testament, heaven is called a *country* (Heb. 11:16). That tells us of its vastness. It is also called a *city* (Heb. 11:10), because of the many inhabitants it will have. It is called a *kingdom* (Matt. 4:17) because of its orderliness, and it is called *paradise* (Luke 23:43) because of its beauty. But what I like best is when Christ calls heaven "my Father's house." As a child, whenever I traveled away from home, I thought the best thing I could possibly do was go back to my father's house. Going to heaven won't be like going into a giant palace where we have to be formal. When we go there, it will be like going home.

In John 2:16, Jesus calls the Temple in Jerusalem His Father's house. When He cleanses the Temple of merchants and moneychangers in Matthew 21:12-13, He says, "Ye have made [My house] a den of thieves" (v. 13). The Temple was the Father's house until Matthew 23:38, where Jesus weeps over Jerusalem and says, "Behold, your house is left unto you desolate." From then on, heaven became the Father's house.

2. The layout of our future home

Jesus said that in His Father's house "are many dwelling places" (John 14:2, NASB*). Some Bible translations use the phrase "many mansions." However, that gives the incorrect idea. We tend to visualize a new real estate development with an agent who shows us a map and says, "Your mansion is two blocks down and four

New American Standard Bible.

15

blocks to the left." But heaven won't be like that. The phrase "dwelling places" refers to how the Israelites lived. When a son became married, the father would add a wing to his house. When another son married, another wing was added. Eventually the original dwelling would become a set of dwellings that enclosed a patio in the middle. All the relatives lived around that patio. So Jesus wasn't talking about a tenement house but a complete dwelling place surrounding a central patio. We will be in dwellings attached to the Father's house—right in the same house with the Father.

Will there be enough room for those who are going to heaven? Jesus said that in His Father's house are *many* dwelling places. There's an old hymn entitled "Plenty Good Room in My Father's House." There will be no overcrowding in heaven; no weary traveler will be turned away. There won't be any No Vacancy signs. God's house is as wide as His love; there will be plenty of room.

Revelation 21:16 tells us how large the city in heaven will be: "The city lieth foursquare, and the length is as large as the breadth; and [an angel] measured the city with the reed, twelve thousand furlongs. The length and the breadth and the height of it are equal." That description gives us a cube with equal sides of approximately 15,000 miles in every direction. An Australian engineer calculated that would be 2,250,000 square miles. To give you a reference point, London is 140 square miles. At the ratio of population in London, the heavenly city could hold 100 billion people. It could hold even more than thirty times the population of our world right now and still have plenty of room to spare!

3. The life-style in our future home

Revelation 21 describes what heaven will be like. In verses 1-4 we read, "I saw a new heaven and a new earth; for the first heaven and the first earth were passed away, and there was no more sea. And I, John, saw the holy city, new Jerusalem, coming down from God out of heaven, prepared as a bride adorned for her husband. And I heard a great voice out of heaven saying,

Behold, the tabernacle of God is with men, and he will dwell with them, and they shall be his people, and God himself shall be with them, and be their God. And God shall wipe away all tears from their eyes; and there shall be no more death, neither sorrow, nor crying, neither shall there be any more pain; for the former things are passed away." When we are in the Father's house, the Lord will take care of all the hurts and needs of His children. He will drive away all pain.

We should already feel bound to heaven. Our Father is there, as well as our Savior, our home, our names, our future lives, our affections, our hearts, our inheritances, and our citizenship. And the great promise of John 14:3 is that Christ is in heaven now preparing it for us!

4. The looks of our future home

There has never been and never will be an interior and exterior decorator like Jesus. Revelation 21:18 says, "The building of the wall of it was of jasper; and the city was pure gold, like clear glass." Have you ever seen pure gold as clear as glass? It doesn't exist, but the Lord will make it. The passage continues, "The foundations of the wall of the city were garnished with all manner of precious stones. The first foundation was jasper; the second, sapphire; the third, chalcedony; the fourth, emerald; the fifth, sardonyx; the sixth, sardius; the seventh, chrysolite; the eighth, beryl; the ninth, topaz; the tenth, chrysoprasus; the eleventh, jacinth; the twelfth, amethyst. And the twelve gates were twelve pearls; each one of the gates was of one pearl; and I saw no temple in it; for the Lord God Almighty and the Lamb are the temple of it. And the city had no need of the sun, neither of the moon, to shine in it; for the glory of God did light it, and the Lamb is the lamp of it" (vv. 19-23). Can't you just imagine the glory of God lighting that city and glittering through all the jewels that stud the walls?

The gates of the city will never be shut (v. 25). Verse 27 says, "There shall in no way enter into it anything that defileth, neither he that worketh abomination, or maketh a lie, but they who are written in the Lamb's book of life." What a city it will be! It will have transparent gold walls studded with jewels that sparkle from the Lamb's glory. There will be no defilement there. And Jesus is getting it ready for us.

B. The Plan to Receive Us (v. 3)

Christ comforts the disciples with these words in John 14:3: "If I go and prepare a place for you, I will come again, and receive you unto myself, that where I am, there ye may be also."

1. The Lord's promise

Not only is Christ preparing heaven for us, but He will also come back and take us there. The Lord isn't going to send someone else to get us. He will take us home personally. That tells us how precious we are to Him.

My dad used to tell a story about a father who dropped off his little boy at a street corner and told him he would be back in twenty minutes after taking care of some business. The father's car broke down, and he wasn't able to get back to his son for four or five hours. The son waited on the corner by a store that whole time, and the panicky father had no way of phoning him. He didn't get back until eleven o'clock at night, and the boy was rocking back and forth on the sidewalk whistling a tune. The father pulled up to the curb, hugged his son, and said he was very sorry. The boy replied, "What are you sorry about? You said you were coming."

That's the kind of trust we can put in the Lord. He said He was coming back. It may look as if it's becoming dark around us and that He may have forgotten, but we can still trust His promise to return. He is getting heaven ready for us, and He is coming to get us.

2. The Lord's desire

It's exciting to know that Jesus is just as anxious to come get us as we are to go to heaven. In John 17:24 He prays, "Father, I will that they also, whom thou hast given me, be with me where I am, that they may behold my glory." Jesus wants us in heaven with Him. When He was here on earth, He told His disciples He wouldn't forsake them, and He says so again in John 14:3.

III. TRUST IN CHRIST'S PERSON (vv. 4-6)

Jesus told the disciples, "Where I go ye know, and the way ye know" (John 14:4). In John 7:33 He tells them He will return to the Father.

A. The Inquiry

Thomas, speaking for all the disciples, said, "Lord, we know not where thou goest; and how can we know the way?" (v. 5). Jesus said He was going to the Father, and Thomas essentially responded, "We don't know what happens to us after death. We don't have any maps on how to get to the Father. How will we understand anything after death?" Thomas had a legitimate concern.

B. The Instruction

Jesus answers his question in verse 6 by saying, "I am the way, the truth, and the life." We don't need to know how to get to heaven; Jesus is coming to get us. We are to trust Him. He is the way. When the right time comes, He will take us by the hand and lead us right to the Father's house.

If you were to go into a strange town and ask for directions, it would be better to have someone lead you to your destination than explain how to get there. That's what Jesus is going to do. Instead of giving us directions, He will take us to the Father's house. Don't worry about what will happen at death or the rapture. Jesus will come back for you.

C. The Insurance

Eighteenth-century pastor Augustus Toplady, who died at the age of thirty-eight in London, was the author of these immortal words in the hymn "Rock of Ages":

> Rock of ages, cleft for me,
> Let me hide myself in Thee;
> Let the water and the blood,
> From Thy wounded side which flowed,
> Be of sin the double cure,
> Save from wrath and make me pure.

When Toplady was near death, he rejoiced and said, "It is my dying avowal that these great and glorious truths, which the Lord in rich mercy has given me to believe and enabled me to preach, are now brought into practical and heartfelt experience. They are the very joy and support of my soul. The consolations flowing from them carry me far above the things of time and sense."

Jesus is the way, the truth, and the life (John 14:6). He is the way to the Father. He is life that is eternal, and He is everything anyone ever needs. Everything that was lost in Adam is regained in Christ. Trust His presence, His promises, and His person. No matter how bad things may become, we have comfort because we can trust Him.

Focusing on the Facts

1. What is the basic theme of John 14 (see p. 8)?
2. In John 14, what emotional state were the disciples in? Why (see p. 9)?
3. What makes Christ stand out as unique among men in John 14 (see p. 9)?

4. What does the basis of comfort come from? Why did the disciples become anxious when the Lord said He would leave them (see pp. 10-11)?
5. What did Isaiah say about our Lord's ability to comfort us (see p. 11)?
6. Explain what Jesus was saying when He said, "Ye believe in God, believe also in me" (John 14:1; see p. 12).
7. What Scriptures in the New Testament assure us of Christ's continual presence in our lives (see p. 13)?
8. In John 16:13-14, Jesus promises to send the Holy Spirit to us. How does the Spirit minister to us (see p. 13)?
9. What promise does Christ give the disciples in John 14:2 (see p. 14)?
10. Where is the Father's house? What are some other scriptural names for the location of our future home, and what is their significance (see p. 15)?
11. How will our dwelling places in the Father's house be laid out (see pp. 15-16)?
12. What does Revelation 21:1-4 tell us about life in heaven (see pp. 16-18)?
13. What promise is given by Christ in John 14:3 (see p. 18)?
14. What desire does Christ express in John 17:24 (see p. 19)?
15. In John 14:5 Thomas says the disciples don't know how to get to heaven after they die. What assurance does Christ give in verse 6 (see p. 19)?

Pondering the Principles

1. The disciples initially viewed Christ's death as a tragic event. They didn't see the good that would come from it. Many people today think Christ died as a martyr, failing to recognize the purpose of His death. According to Romans 3:25-26 and 2 Corinthians 5:21, what did Christ's death accomplish for us? Over what did Christ achieve victory (Heb. 2:14)? What can we receive as a result of Christ's death (John 16:7, 13; 1 Pet. 1:3-4)? God's master plan for the salvation and glorification of man required a perfect sacrifice. That sacrifice was Christ. What appears to be a tragic event in history, then, is actually the greatest victory for all mankind. Praise the Lord for that great victory on our behalf.

2. It's easy for us to be preoccupied with the problems and issues of the moment and forget about the wondrous joys that await us in eternity. Take a few minutes now to meditate on Revelation 21:1—22:5. What are some things you have to look forward to in your new home? How will life be different from what it is now? Thinking about your future home frequently will give you an eternal and refreshing perspective that results in giving thanks and praise to God.

2

Jesus Is God

Outline

Introduction

Lesson
I. The Revelation of Christ's Person (vv. 7-11)
   A. The Reaffirmation (v. 7)
      1. Pointing out a lack of understanding (v. 7a)
      2. Promising a full understanding (v. 7b)
         a) The argument for immediate understanding
         b) The argument for eventual understanding
   B. The Request (v. 8)
   C. The Response (vv. 9-11)
      1. The confrontation about Christ's deity (v. 9a)
      2. The claim regarding Christ's deity (v. 9b)
      3. The command regarding Christ's deity (v. 10a)
      4. The confirmation of Christ's deity (vv. 10b-11)
         a) Through His words (v. 10b)
            (1) John 3:34
            (2) John 12:49
            (3) Matthew 7:28-29
         b) Through His works (vv. 10c-11)
II. The Revelation of Christ's Power (v. 12)
   A. Explaining the Prerequisite
   B. Examining the Power
      1. Physical works
      2. Spiritual works
III. The Revelation of Christ's Promise (vv. 13-14)
   A. The Anxiety over Provisions
   B. The Assurance of Provisions

Conclusion

Introduction

John 14:7-14 describes an important moment in the life of any follower of Jesus Christ. In those verses are some of the most amazing things Jesus ever said. Christ's claim to be God is staggering, and His statement that we will do greater things than He did is also incredible. Even more monumental is His concluding statement that whatever we ask in His name, He will do it. So John 14:7-14 not only declares who Jesus is but also states what Jesus will do through those who belong to Him.

We will never comprehend the fullness of what John 14:7-14 says until we have perfect knowledge in heaven. But we will try to learn as much as we can from those verses. Before we do so, let me give you some background information and set the scene.

The events in John 14 took place on the night before Christ's crucifixion. Many things transpired in the course of His three-year ministry, and now He was about to die. On that last evening Jesus gave His last address to eleven of His disciples. Judas was dismissed in John 13 to carry out his betrayal. The Lord's last hours with the disciples were crucial because He had to prepare them for the traumatic shock they would soon experience when He died. He taught them, showed His love for them, and gave them commands and promises. He shared His final words with them.

Lesson

John 14 is the comfort chapter of the New Testament. We've already seen how Jesus comforts the disciples in the first six verses by telling them He will come back for them. He explained He was leaving them so He could prepare a place for them. Then in verses 7-14 the Lord continues to comfort the disciples by giving them three great revelations: the revelation of His person, the revelation of His power, and the revelation of His promise. Although Jesus had already stated different aspects of those revelations to the disciples in the past, they took on a new meaning because He was soon to leave them.

I. THE REVELATION OF CHRIST'S PERSON (vv. 7-11)

Christ found it necessary to reaffirm who He was because the disciples were trying to figure out how He could be the Messiah if He had to die. They were wondering why He couldn't defend Himself not only against a hostile world, but against one disciple who would deny Him and another who would betray Him. Christ knew what the disciples were thinking, so He revealed His Person to them in a new way. What did Jesus reveal about Himself? He revealed that He was God.

An Indisputable, Unavoidable Claim

Christ's claim to be God has been debated throughout history. Everyone who studies about Christ encounters His claim to be God. Some people conclude that Jesus is a madman who had delusions of grandeur. Others conclude He was a fraud, and some say He was simply a good teacher. (That third option isn't possible because a good teacher wouldn't claim to be God.) And finally, there are some who say that Christ indeed is God. But the issue is: Is Christ God or not? Jesus says in John 14 that He is nothing less than God.

How could that information comfort the disciples? In John 14:4, Jesus tells the disciples He is going away and that they know the way to where He is going. What did He mean by that? The disciples knew that Jesus had come from the Father; He had told them that all along. That's why He could say they knew the way to where He was going. But the disciples were probably scratching their heads in confusion, and Thomas said, "Lord, we know not where thou goest; and how can we know the way?" (v. 5). Jesus responded, "I am the way, the truth, and the life; no man cometh unto the Father, but by me" (v. 6).

The disciples were still confused. They were probably thinking, *What does God look like, and how do we get to Him? How does a person find his way to the Father after he dies? We don't know where He is or what He looks like.* Jesus said He was going to the Father and that He would take them to the Father later on (John 14:2-3). But the disciples weren't so sure; their faith wasn't strong. So in their confusion, Jesus told them, "Don't be confused about the Father. If you know Me, you know the Father because I am God."

Jesus reassured the disciples by telling them He was one with the Father. In John 1:14 we read, "The Word was made flesh, and dwelt among us (and we beheld his glory, the glory as of the only begotten of the Father)." Jesus Christ is God. With that in mind, let's look at the dialogue from verse 7 on.

A. The Reaffirmation (v. 7)

1. Pointing out a lack of understanding (v. 7a)

"If ye had known me, ye should have known my Father also."

Jesus was telling the disciples, "If you really knew Me, you wouldn't be worried about who the Father is." The disciples didn't have full knowledge of who Jesus was. However, they had confessed that He was the Messiah, the anointed of God. Peter said that Jesus was "the Son of the living God" (Matt. 16:16), recognizing His deity. But Peter did not come to that conclusion on his own; Jesus said that truth was revealed to Peter by the Father (Matt. 16:17).

Even though the disciples had a basic knowledge of Jesus, their knowledge was limited. That's why Jesus said that if they really knew Him, they would know the Father also. If the disciples were so unsure about the Father, it was because there were loopholes in their knowledge about Christ. If they fully knew Jesus, they would have fully known God. They would not have been worried when Jesus said He was going to the Father to prepare a place for them. They wouldn't have worried about getting the directions to reach the Father. The disciples' anxiety resulted from their failing to see Jesus fully as God. That's why they had their fears and doubts.

Jesus is making a substantial claim in John 14:7. In verse 6 He says He is the way to God, the truth about God, and the life of God. Now He says He is God. Keep in mind that He isn't a manifestation of God; He is God in the flesh. The Sabellian heresy taught that Jesus was just a manifestation of God—that He merely possessed the essence of God and wasn't really the eternal God Himself. But He is God manifest—there's a big difference between the two. So Christ told the disciples that He is God, and He makes that more evident in the verses following. The disciples knew Jesus cared for them, and He wanted them to know that God would carry out His love and protection because He and God are One. They didn't need to worry about how to get to God or wonder about the Father, because if they knew Jesus, they also knew the Father.

2. Promising a full understanding (v. 7b)

"From henceforth ye know him, and have seen him."

That's a difficult statement to interpret. It has two possible explanations. I'll give you both and tell you which one I believe is better.

Jesus said, "From now on [that's what *henceforth* means], you know the Father." Earlier in verse 7 He in effect says, "You don't really know Me, so you don't really know the Father." So it seems to make sense that He would next say, "But from now on, you will know Him." The problem is, when does the time "from now on" begin?

a) The argument for immediate understanding

The first possible interpretation is that the disciples would know the Father beginning immediately. That would render Jesus' statement to say, "Men, from this moment on, you will know the Father. I have just said if you knew Me you would know Him. From now on, you will know Him and have everything straight."

There is a problem with that interpretation. Jesus had told them about the Father before without their fully understanding. Why would they necessarily have full understanding here? In fact, they didn't, because in the next verse Philip says, "Lord, show us the Father, and it sufficeth us" (John 14:8). He was saying, "If you show us God, that will help us." He still didn't know who Jesus was. I don't believe the fulfillment of John 14:7b took place at that time, because the disciples are still confused in verse 8.

b) The argument for eventual understanding

The other interpretation involves a close look at the grammar of the Greek text. The Greeks often used tenses that we would consider incorrect in the English language. Sometimes they used the present tense and the past tense to refer to the future. Sometimes when they spoke about future events that were certain to happen, they spoke of them as if they had already taken place. I believe that's what Jesus is doing in John 14:7. He is referring to a time in the future when the disciples would begin to understand the truths concerning Himself. Their eventual understanding was so certain to Him, He could speak of it in the past tense. And during the events of Christ's death, resurrection, and ascension, and the coming of the Holy Spirit, they understood clearly. Some of the disciples were convinced after the resurrection. When Thomas saw Jesus after the resurrection he said, "My Lord and my God" (John 20:28). Yet Thomas didn't understand before the resurrection. At first he didn't even believe Jesus arose. Basically it wasn't until the events that led up to the day of the Pentecost, when the Holy Spirit came to dwell in them permanently, that the disciples had full understanding.

So, Jesus promised the disciples that they would eventually understand about Him and the Father. The Holy Spirit would help them. As we learned in the previous lesson, the Holy Spirit's ministry is to point to Christ and declare who He is. The Spirit did that in the apostles' lives, even as He does in our lives today.

B. The Request (v. 8)

"Philip saith unto him, Lord, show us the Father, and it sufficeth us."

28

As I said earlier, verse 7 could not have been immediately fulfilled or Philip wouldn't have asked that question. It was a shallow question asked out of ignorance. Philip had heard what Jesus said, but he still didn't understand what Jesus meant. His knowledge of both Christ and God was incomplete. He did what many other people in history have done: he asked for a visible manifestation. That brings up the matter of faith and sight again. It wasn't enough for Philip to believe; he wanted to see the Father.

Perhaps Philip had in mind Exodus 33:22-23, when Moses saw the tail end of God's glory from a cleft in a rock. Or maybe he thought about when Moses, Aaron, Nadab, Abihu, and seventy of the elders of Israel "saw the God of Israel . . . as it were the body of heaven in its clearness" (Ex. 24:10). Philip may have recalled Isaiah 40:5, which says, "The glory of the Lord shall be revealed, and all flesh shall see it together." But in John 14:8, Philip shows he is a faithless disciple who wants sight to substitute for faith. He wanted Jesus to back up what He was saying with full visible proof.

Philip was basically saying, "If You are leaving, and things are going to become bad for us, then couldn't You show us the Father so that we know You're not kidding us? How can we be sure You're really going to the Father's house to prepare us a place, and that You're going to come get us? Can't the Father come and confirm all those things?" Philip's statement shows his lack of faith. His belief that Jesus was God and his security were dependent on sight.

The other disciples also showed their lack of trust in Christ. In Acts 1:10-11, when they stare as the Lord ascended all the way up into heaven, two angels ask them, "Ye men of Galilee, why stand ye gazing up into heaven?" (v. 11). I sometimes wonder if when they were watching Christ ascend, they were hoping to see how to go to the Father. They may have been afraid that once Jesus was gone, they would be deserted without any way of getting to the Father. Philip tried to clear up his fear by asking Jesus to show the Father to the disciples. The sight of God would be like a pledge that the future Jesus promised them really did await them. Yet depending on sight is typical of one who has little faith.

C. The Response (vv. 9-11)

1. The confrontation about Christ's deity (v. 9*a*)

   "Jesus saith unto him, Have I been such a long time
   with you, and yet hast thou not known me, Philip?"

   What a statement! I believe Jesus was rebuking Philip as
   well as displaying deep emotion. Can you imagine how
   heartbroken Jesus was when after three years of inten-
   sive teaching, one disciple turned out to be a traitor, another a swearing denier, and the other ten were men of
   little faith? How discouraged He must have been! Yet
   here they were, the night before His death, and they still
   didn't know who He was. It's sad to realize that after all
   the repeated displays of Christ's deity, the disciples still
   didn't get the message. And it wasn't easy for Jesus to
   make those men disciples; they had been difficult to
   work with all along. Don't feel bad if you become discouraged about someone you disciple. Jesus experienced such discouragement.

2. The claim regarding Christ's deity (v. 9*b*)

   "He that hath seen me hath seen the Father; and how
   sayest thou then, Show us the Father?"

   Jesus could have said that only if He really was God;
   otherwise He could be labeled a lunatic. Jesus was telling Philip, "Here you are looking Me in the face, and
   asking Me to show you God. Open your eyes; you've
   been looking at Him for three years!" The writer of Hebrews said that Jesus is the express image of God's Person (Heb. 1:3). The apostle Paul says in Colossians 1:15
   that Jesus is the image of the invisible God. In Colossians 2:9 he says that in Christ "dwelleth all the fullness
   of the Godhead bodily." It must have been painful for
   Jesus to hear that the disciples still didn't know who He
   was, even after pouring His life into them for three
   years!

   Discipleship can be heartbreaking. I can think of people
   whom I had the privilege of leading to Christ and disci-
   pling for one, two, or even three years with little or noth-

ing to show for it. That will happen sometimes, and it is tragic. Do you know what Jesus did when He was faced with that? He did all He could for the disciples, then turned everything over to the Holy Spirit (John 16:7). That's a good principle to remember in discipleship. You work with someone as long as you can and then move on.

3. The command regarding Christ's deity (v. 10a)

"Believest thou not that I am in the Father, and the Father in me?"

When Philip said, "Show us the Father," Jesus responded by simply saying, "Believe." He didn't do any special tricks or display the Father. In verse 11, again He says to believe in Him. Philip asked for visual evidence, and Jesus told him to have faith. That's what Christianity is all about: believing.

I have never seen Jesus. I have never heard voices from heaven. I have never seen a dead person rise again. I have never seen God with my own eyes, yet there is nothing I know any surer than that God, Christ, and the Holy Spirit are real. My spiritual eyes perceive things my physical eyes could never see. Christianity is all about believing, not seeing. It does not deal strictly with visible miracles and strange phenomena. I don't want visions and ecstatic events to confirm God for me; I just want what the disciples asked of the Lord in Luke 17:5: "Increase our faith." It's by faith that we perceive God. Jesus operates on faith, and the Bible is a book of faith.

After three years with Jesus, Philip—and perhaps the other disciples—didn't have sufficient faith to settle their troubled hearts just by believing. They had to have a visible sign. No wonder Jesus often referred to them as men of little faith! What exactly is faith? Someone once defined it as believing in something you know isn't so. But in reality, faith is the opposite: it is believing in something that you know is so. Faith has evidence. In the latter part of John 14:10 Jesus gives Philip the evidence for faith.

31

4. The confirmation of Christ's deity (vv. 10b-11)

   a) Through His words (v. 10b)

   "The words that I speak unto you, I speak not of myself."

   Jesus was saying, "Philip, have you listened to what I have said to you for the last three years?" What exactly did Jesus say? Here is a sampling from Scripture:

   (1) John 3:34

   John the Baptist said of Jesus, "He whom God hath sent speaketh the words of God; for God giveth not the Spirit by measure unto him." The things Jesus said were right from the mouth of God.

   (2) John 12:49

   Jesus said, "I have not spoken of myself; but the Father, who sent me, he gave me a commandment, what I should say, and what I should speak."

   (3) Matthew 7:28-29

   Here we find a great illustration of the power of the words of Jesus: "It came to pass, when Jesus had ended these sayings, the people were astonished at his doctrine; for he taught them as one having authority, and not as the scribes."

   The words of Jesus ought to be enough to penetrate the mind and heart of any man and elicit faith. His profession to be the great I AM of Exodus 3:14 (John 8:58), His teachings, and His innate knowledge of the human heart should be enough to make people place their faith in Him as the true God. He answered questions before people were able to ask them. The faith of Christians is based on the words of Jesus.

b) Through His works (vv. 10*c*-11)

> "The Father that dwelleth in me, he doeth the works. Believe me that I am in the Father, and the Father in me; or else believe me for the very works' sake."

If Jesus' words weren't sufficient proof of His deity, then His works would be. The disciples had seen Him do many miracles. In John 5:36 Jesus says, "I have greater witness than that of John; for the works which the Father hath given me to finish, the same works that I do, bear witness of me, that the Father hath sent me." He gave the same testimony in John 10:25. So Jesus was saying in John 14:10-11, "You don't need to see anything, Philip. What am I going to show you? I am God manifest. Believe My words and My works."

The Lord revealed to the disciples the tremendous truth that He is God. That should have been a source of comfort for them. If they would believe that, they would be able to rest easy knowing that they were secure in Him.

II. THE REVELATION OF CHRIST'S POWER (v. 12)

"Verily, verily, I say unto you, He that believeth on me, the works that I do shall he do also; and greater works than these shall he do, because I go unto my Father."

A. Explaining the Prerequisite

The key to the astounding promise in John 14:12 is the phrase "because I go unto my Father." The only way the disciples would be able to do the works Jesus did and even greater works was if He went to the Father. Why? Because it wasn't until Jesus went to the Father that the Holy Spirit was sent.

B. Examining the Power

When the Holy Spirit came, the disciples were empowered to do tremendous miracles throughout the known world. They were able to do what Christ did and even greater things, not in power but in extent. That shows us why it's better to have the Holy Spirit indwelling every believer than to have Christ present on earth. Every Christian has the resident power of deity in the indwelling Spirit. That's why Christ was able to tell the disciples that they would do even greater things than He did. What a promise! The disciples were discouraged when Christ said He was leaving because they thought they were going to be reduced to nothing. But Jesus said they would be empowered to do greater things.

When Jesus said the disciples would do greater things than He did, He basically referred to the extent of their ministry, not the power they would have. No one could do any works greater in power than what Jesus did. But the extent of the disciples' ministry was much greater. For example, Jesus had never preached outside of Palestine. The disciples made far more converts than Jesus ever made.

1. Physical works

   The promise Jesus gives in John 14:12 refers to the ability to do miracles. The disciples were empowered by the indwelling Holy Spirit to do miracles. In Acts 3, Peter and John heal a lame man. In Acts 5 we read, "By the hands of the apostles were many signs and wonders wrought among the people. . . . Insomuch that they brought forth the sick into the streets, and laid them on beds and couches, that at least the shadow of Peter passing by might overshadow some of them. There came also a multitude out of the cities round about unto Jerusalem, bringing sick folks, and them who were vexed with unclean spirits; and they were healed every one" (vv. 12, 15-16). Hebrews 2:3-4 tells us that God bore witness with the apostles through signs, wonders, and diverse miracles and gifts of the Holy Spirit. The apostles were able to do the same miracles Jesus did. They had the same power.

2. Spiritual works

   Although the apostles had the same power to do physical works as Jesus did, they did greater things spiritually. When Peter preached to the crowd in Acts 2, three thousand people became saved (v. 41). Did that ever happen during Jesus' ministry? No, and neither did the gospel go to the Gentiles. That didn't happen until Peter visited Cornelius in Acts 10 and Paul preached the gospel to Gentiles all over Europe. Now it wasn't that Jesus couldn't do those things; the Lord simply designed to not do them. He chose to work through His apostles. Some time ago while I was in Israel, I couldn't help but keep thinking of how small the country is. The sphere of Jesus' ministry was small, and there weren't many people then. But now, we see spiritual miracles happening every minute all over the world. Those spiritual miracles are being done by believers through the power of the indwelling Spirit. And the greatest spiritual miracle of all is salvation. We are witnesses to the new birth every time we introduce someone to Christ.

Can We Do the Same Mighty Works the Apostles Did?

The promise in John 14:12 was primarily directed to the disciples. We are able to do great spiritual works but not physical works. We can't heal sick people. James 5:14 gives instructions on what to do when someone is sick and doesn't mention anything about trying to heal people: "Call for the elders of the church; and let them pray over him, anointing him with oil in the name of the Lord." To anoint someone with oil was to give them some medicine. In Luke 10, the Good Samaritan pours oil on the wounds of the injured traveler. James 5:15 says, "The prayer of faith shall save the sick." We can see God heal by prayer. By the time James wrote that, which was around 50 A.D., the early church knew that the ability to heal had belonged only to the apostles. James didn't say a sick person should seek a healer; he said to have the church elders pray for him. The age of miracles was over because the Word of God was becoming complete. The miraculous gifts were only to confirm that the apostles were of God before the Word was complete.

Although the ability to do miraculous physical works was restricted to the apostles, it's marvelous to see spiritual miracles happening in our own lives as we minister. It's exciting to be involved in what God is doing spiritually and to be doing even greater things than what happened in Jesus' day. Did you know there was never a revival during Christ's ministry on earth? Yet since that time we have seen great revivals in Scotland, Ireland, England, America, Korea, and Indonesia. Revivals are still going on today. You and I are in the midst of great spiritual miracles, and it's because Jesus returned to the Father and sent the Holy Spirit.

III. THE REVELATION OF CHRIST'S PROMISE (vv. 13-14)

"And whatever ye shall ask in my name, that will I do, that the Father may be glorified in the Son. If ye shall ask anything in my name, I will do it."

A. The Anxiety over Provisions

When Jesus told the disciples He would leave them, I'm sure they were thinking, *Where are we going to go for our resources?* Christ had fed them and taken care of them. He helped them catch fish (Luke 5:4-6) and on one occasion even provided tax money from the mouth of a fish (Matt. 17:27). But now Jesus was going away, and the disciples knew the world didn't like them. How were they going to get jobs? How were they going to fit back into society? They had no resources; they feared having to be all alone.

B. The Assurance of Provisions

While the disciples were having those thoughts, Jesus said, "Men, I may be gone, but whatever you need, ask Me and I'll provide it." That's a fantastic promise! The gap between where Christ is and where we are is closed instantly as we pray. Paul said, "My God shall supply all your need according to his riches in glory by Christ Jesus" (Phil. 4:19).

Is Your Prayer List Like a Santa Claus List?

Can we ask God for anything we want? Is Jesus' statement in John 14:13-14 carte blanche for every whim of the flesh? No; there is a qualifying statement made twice in John 14:13-14: "in my name." Those three words qualify every prayer God answers. What does it mean to ask for something in the Lord's name? Some people think it means to say, "In the name of Jesus. Amen," at the end of their prayers. That's not what Christ was referring to. He meant:

1. We're to acknowledge Christ's person

   To speak of the name of Jesus is to acknowledge all that He is and all that He did. When we pray in Christ's name, it's as if Christ Himself were making the request. By praying in His name, you are fully identifying with Him. It would be like saying, "Father, I ask that You do this for Jesus' sake." Having that perspective helps eliminate selfish prayers.

2. We're to bring before God the merits of His Son

   To pray in Christ's name is to say, "Father, here's my request. Give it to me because of all that Jesus has done."

3. We're to pray only for what is consistent with Christ's glory

   Here's a practical test you can use when you make requests to God: say, "Father, I'm asking this because I know it will bring glory to Jesus." You can't ask God for a new television set and say that it will glorify Christ. Using that test will help you pray for the things that really matter. And at the end of verse 14 Jesus says, "I will do it." He didn't say, "All right, guys, that's your request—now carry it out." He said He would grant our requests. Jesus answers our prayers.

Conclusion

Now you can see how Jesus lovingly comforts His disciples in John 14:7-14. He gave them the revelation of His person, His power, and His promise. What a comfort to know that He cares! Our prayer should be the same as that of the disciples in Luke 17:5. We shouldn't ask, "Lord, show me such-and-such," but, "Increase my faith to believe You so that I can see You at work in my life."

Focusing on the Facts

1. Why did Christ find it necessary to reaffirm to the disciples who He was (see p. 25)?
2. Did the disciples have full knowledge of who Jesus was? Explain (see pp. 25-26).
3. What are the two explanations of Jesus' statement "From henceforth ye know him, and have seen him" (John 14:7)? Which seems to be the better explanation, and why (see pp. 27-28)?
4. When did the disciples fully understand who Jesus was (see p. 28)?
5. Explain what Philip was asking Christ in John 14:8 (see p. 29).
6. What did Philip's statement show about his faith? What was his belief in Jesus dependent upon (see p. 29)?
7. When Jesus rebuked Philip by His statement in John 14:9, why was our Lord heartbroken (see p. 30)?
8. What does Scripture say about Christ's deity (see p. 30)?
9. What principle should you keep in mind when you disciple someone (see p. 31)?
10. What did Jesus tell Philip to do when asked to show the Father (John 14:10-11; see p. 31)?
11. What did the disciples ask the Lord for in Luke 17:5? Why should that be all we want (see p. 31)?
12. In John 14:10, Jesus says that the words He spoke were not His own. What other Scriptures support that statement, and what do they say (see p. 32)?
13. Other than by His words, how else did Christ confirm His deity (see p. 33)?
14. What had to happen before the disciples would be able to do the great things Christ had done (see p. 33)?
15. What was Jesus referring to when He said the disciples would do greater things than He did (see p. 34)?
16. Describe the physical works the apostles did, supporting your answer with Scripture (see pp. 34).
17. In what way did the apostles do a greater spiritual work than what Christ did (see pp. 34-35)?
18. To whom was the promise in John 14:12 primarily directed? Explain (see p. 35).
19. What great promise did Christ make in John 14:13-14? How is that promise qualified (see pp. 36-37)?
20. The gap between where Christ is and where we are is _____ instantly as we _____ (see p. 36).

Pondering the Principles

1. There are many cults today that deny Christ is God, and there are some people who say He was simply a great man. However, Scripture is clear about the true identity of Christ. In John 8:58-59, some Jewish religious leaders want to stone Christ for claiming to be the great I AM (cf. Ex. 3:14). Read the following verses: Isaiah 9:6; John 10:30-33; 20:28; Colossians 1:15-19; 2:9; Titus 2:13. How is Christ's deity affirmed in those verses? When a person denies Christ is God, he isn't recognizing Christ for all that He is and is perverting the truth. Memorize the verse references above or write them down inside the cover of your Bible so that you will always be ready to respond to those who say Christ is not God.

2. Because Christ is God, we know He can keep His promises and that He is sovereign. He has conquered death and can cleanse us of our sins. He can meet both our spiritual and physical needs. Someday, He will reign as King of kings and Lord of lords. In what ways do those truths comfort you? Share your thoughts with the Lord in a time of prayer and praise.

3. Christ promised the disciples that He would continue to meet their needs after He left them, and told them to present their needs to Him in prayer. We only need to keep in mind that the prayer requests we make are to be consistent with what Christ would want and with what would glorify Him. Memorize Christ's great promise in John 14:13-14: "Whatever you ask in My name, that will I do, that the Father may be glorified in the Son. If you ask Me anything in My name, I will do it" (NASB).

3

Sorrow Turned to Joy

Outline

Introduction

Lesson
I. The Pledge (v. 16)
  A. Clarifying the Pledge
  B. Clarifying a Phrase
    1. The first "little while"
    2. The second "little while"
      a) What it is not
        (1) The second coming
        (2) The resurrection
      b) What it is
        (1) The explanation
        (2) The evidence
        (3) The event
II. The Perplexity (vv. 17-19)
  A. The Stirring (v. 17)
  B. The Silence (v. 18)
    1. Christ's desire to share with the disciples
    2. Christ's approach to comforting the disciples
  C. The Surprise (v. 19)
III. The Parable (vv. 20-22)
  A. The Instruction (v. 20)
    1. The prediction
    2. The principle
      a) In relation to the disciples
      b) In relation to us
  B. The Illustration
    1. Initial sorrow (v. 21a)
    2. Inevitable joy (v. 21b)

Introduction

The greatest word that could ever be said to a person in sorrow would be the promise that his sorrow will be temporary. From John 13 to John 16, Jesus comforts His sorrowful disciples on the night before His death. He alleviated their sorrow with promises, wonderful hopes, and the assurance of His presence through the Holy Spirit. He told them they would do greater things than He did (John 14:12), and that they could ask anything in His name and it would be granted (John 14:13-14). In John 15 He says they will have the power to be victorious over the hateful world and that they will be His witnesses. Yet, in John 16 the disciples are still sorrowful.

Jesus told the disciples that He understood their sorrow. Twice in John 14 He says, "Let not your heart be troubled" (vv. 1, 27). In John 16:6 the Lord acknowledges the sorrow that filled the disciples' hearts. He knew they were grieving over the prospect of losing Him. They simply didn't understand much of what Christ was saying about His physical death and departure. So in John 14-16, Jesus turns His thoughts and concerns toward the disciples and endeavors to comfort them. In this lesson, we will look at how He climaxes His message of comfort with the statement that soon their sorrow would be turned to joy, because His departure was only temporary.

Lesson

I have divided John 16:16-24 into four points: the pledge, the perplexity, the parable, and the promise. What is amazing about Christ's actions is that He unselfishly comforted the disciples at a time when He could have been preoccupied with what was going to happen to Him at the cross. He anticipated what was about to happen to Him yet pushed aside any thoughts of Himself and condescended to minister to the sorrow of the selfish disciples. He stooped to their weakness because He loved them.

I. THE PLEDGE (v. 16)

"A little while, and ye shall not see me; and again, a little while, and ye shall see me, because I go to the Father."

A. Clarifying the Pledge

Initially, that statement may seem confusing. It doesn't immediately make sense. Examining the statement piece by piece will help us understand it. First the Lord said, "A little while, and ye shall not see me." We can understand that statement because it was spoken about two or three hours before the arrest of Jesus and the events that led to the cross. The disciples would see Him for a little longer, and then He would be out of their midst.

Then Jesus said, "Again, a little while, and ye shall see me." He was ministering in the simplest way possible to the discouraged disciples. He said, "It's true that I'm going away, but it's only temporary. In a little while I will be back." He gave them hope, which offered the greatest possible alleviation of sorrow.

Everyone in the church, the Body of Christ, should concern himself with others—not himself. Jesus wasn't preoccupied with Himself; He didn't worry about the things that must have been tearing His heart to pieces. He didn't dwell on the anguish He would experience when He bore the sins of the world and endured the hatred that was to come. He stopped any thought of Himself and considered the sorrow of the undeserving, selfish disciples.

B. Clarifying a Phrase

To fully understand what Jesus was saying in John 16:16, we need to consider the key phrase that appears twice in the verse: "a little while." Jesus had used the phrase before to refer to weeks, days, and hours. In John 7:33 He says, "Yet a little while am I with you, and then I go unto him that sent me." At that time, His departure was only weeks away. In John 12:35 He says, "Yet a little while is the light with you. Walk while ye have the light, lest darkness come upon you." There, the phrase "a little while" refers to days. Then in John 13:33 we read, "Little children, yet a little while I am with you." At that point it was only a matter of hours before Christ's arrest. By the time we get to John 16, Jesus uses the same phrase again to refer to two or three hours.

Based on those verses, the phrase "a little while" can refer to any amount of time from a few weeks to a few hours. We use that same phrase today to mean basically the same thing.

1. The first "little while"

The first time Jesus used the phrase "a little while" in John 16:16 refers to the hours before Jesus went to the Garden of Gethsemane, where He was arrested. Some commentators believe that in John 16 Jesus is actually en route to the Garden, having already left the upper room. Regardless, His disciples would be separated from Him in as little as two hours. In fact, they would flee. Then Jesus said, "Again, a little while, and ye shall see me, because I go to the Father." When were the disciples going to see Jesus again? What was He referring to?

2. The second "little while"

   a) What it is not

      (1) The second coming

         Some people say Christ was talking about His second coming. He would be gone for a while and then return at the second coming. They support that interpretation by pointing to the New Testament reference that depicts the period prior to Christ's return as being the birth pangs of the coming kingdom (Matt. 24:8). Since Jesus used the metaphor of birth a little later on in verse 21 to illustrate what He was saying, some people say the second "little while" must refer to the second coming—that there will be birth pangs experienced during the Tribulation, and then the kingdom will come.

I don't believe that's the right interpretation because Christ is coming to get us at the rapture, which will happen before the second coming. We won't remain on earth until He sets up His kingdom at the second coming; we will be raptured seven years before that. In John 14:2-3 Jesus says He is going to heaven to prepare a place for us, and that He will come to take us where He is. To say the disciples would next see Him at the second coming would eliminate the pretribulation rapture. It would also give them small comfort to say, "I'll be leaving you in a couple of hours, but I'll be back in two thousand years. So, be comforted." Finally, it wouldn't be consistent to interpret "a little while" to mean a few hours in one place and two thousand years in another.

(2) The resurrection

Some people say the second "little while" refers to the resurrection. Now that seems more possible, because three days can be considered a "little while." Jesus uses the phrase "a little while" to refer to a few days in John 12:35 when He says, "A little while is the light with you." However, there's a problem with that interpretation: after Christ's resurrection, He was around for only a few weeks before He left the disciples again. That would be to say, "Don't be afraid. I'm going away but I'll be back in three days. Then I'll go away again." That's not a permanent comfort.

What, then, was Jesus saying? Look at the statement at the end of the verse: "A little while, and ye shall see me, because I go to the Father." How would they be able to see Him when He left to go to the Father?

b) What it is

(1) The explanation

Jesus said that when He went to the Father, He would send the Holy Spirit (John 14:16, 26). According to Romans 8:9, the Holy Spirit is the Spirit of Christ. So when Christ said the disciples would see Him again, He was saying He would be back not in a physical body but through the person of the Spirit. The Holy Spirit would dwell in us (John 14:17). In John 16:7 the Lord says, "Nevertheless, I tell you the truth: It is expedient for you that I go away; for if I go not away, the Comforter will not come unto you." Christ couldn't send His Spirit yet because the Spirit was a reward to Him from the Father for accomplishing the work on the cross (Eph. 1:13-14). When Christ went to heaven having accomplished His work, the Father sent the Spirit, who came in Christ's place.

(2) The evidence

In John 14:16 Christ says, "I will pray the Father, and he shall give you another Comforter." There are two Greek words for the word *another*: *heteros*, which means "another of a different kind," and *allos*, which means "another of the same kind." Christ used *allos*. The Spirit is one in essence with Him; Christ would be sending back His own Spirit. That is confirmed in John 14:17-18, where Christ says He would send "the Spirit of truth, whom the world cannot receive, because it seeth him not, neither knoweth him: but ye know him; for he dwelleth with you, and shall be in you. I will not leave you comfortless; I will come to you." In verse 17 He says the Spirit will come, then in verse 18 He says He will come. Both verses are talking about the same event; the promised Holy Spirit is the Spirit of Christ.

Paul said Christ in us is the hope of glory (Col. 1:27), and Christ promised His Spirit would reside in us (John 14:17). And He will reside in us permanently. He didn't tell the disciples He would come back and leave again. Nor did He say He would leave and be back in two thousand years. He said He would leave, then come back and be with us as long as we live and throughout eternity. In Matthew 28:20 Christ says, "Lo, I am with you always, even unto the end of the age." He will never leave or forsake us (Heb. 13:5).

(3) The event

The fulfillment of Christ's promise came on the Day of Pentecost (Acts 2:4). The Spirit came and dwelt within the disciples and began to teach them all things concerning Christ, as John 14:26 says He would. Prior to John 16:16, in verses 13-15, Christ details the work of the Father. Then in verse 16 He says that work will begin when He goes to the Father.

Summed up, Christ is saying in John 16:16, "I'm going away, and because I'm going to the Father, I'll come to you in the form of My Spirit to dwell within you." That's a wonderful promise every believer has. There's no such thing as a Christian who doesn't possess the indwelling Christ. There are people who think they have to search for the Holy Spirit, but He dwells in every believer. Paul told the Corinthians, "Know ye not that ye are the temple of God, and that the Spirit of God dwelleth in you?" (1 Cor. 3:16). That's basic knowledge. Christ in us is the hope of glory (Col. 1:27).

Christ pledged that He would return after His temporary departure. And when He returned, it wouldn't be in His physical body, which could be in only one place at a time. He would be in every believer at all times. Sure enough, within a few weeks of making His pledge, the apostles received the Holy Spirit (Acts 2:4). The phrase "a little while" can be used to refer to weeks, so that interpretation is appropriate. The first "little while" talks of hours, and the second speaks of weeks.

Jesus has already left and sent the Spirit. We now live in the age of the Spirit's indwelling every believer. That's what Christ promised would happen. What is it that the Spirit wants to do within us during this age? Manifest Jesus Christ. Christ says in John 16:14 that the Spirit "shall glorify me; for he shall receive of mine, and shall show it unto you." The Spirit's ministry is to manifest Christ within us. That's quite a pledge. By the perceptive eye of faith, we know it has been fulfilled. I've never seen the Holy Spirit, but I know He is present in my life. Through the eye of faith, we perceive His working in our lives. We sense His presence.

By the way, when Christ spoke of the disciples' seeing Him again, He may also have been referring to the resurrection, ascension, and coming of the Spirit as a unit. The cross, resurrection, ascension, and coming of the Spirit were all one climax that began the age of the Spirit.

II. THE PERPLEXITY (vv. 17-19)

The disciples were frequently perplexed by Christ's statements. They usually said, "What does He mean?" It's interesting that in John 16:17 we see the disciples break their silence for the first time since John 14:22. They responded quizzically to Jesus' leaving and returning in a little while. They had just resigned themselves to the fact that He was going to die. Then all of a sudden Christ said they would see Him again after a little while. They must have been thinking, *How does a person die for only a little while?*

A. The Stirring (v. 17)

"Then said some of his disciples among themselves, What is this that he saith unto us, A little while, and ye shall not see me; and again, a little while, and ye shall see me; and, Because I go to the Father?"

The disciples didn't have the courage to ask Jesus what He meant, so they started talking among themselves. They were confused about His saying He was coming back in a little while because He was going to the Father. Now don't be hard on the disciples because they were confused; if we were in their shoes, we would not have understood what Jesus meant prior to the events that happened at the cross and immediately thereafter. They were struggling with the question of how the Messiah could leave if He was supposed to set up His kingdom. They finally understood that He was going to leave them, but what did He mean by saying He would come back?

B. The Silence (v. 18)

"They said, therefore, What is this that he saith, A little while? We cannot tell what he saith."

The disciples were confused, and rather than be rebuked for not understanding, they chose to remain silent. That's a shame; there are some people like that in Sunday school classes or Bible study groups. They can't understand what's being said and are afraid to ask any questions because they think they will appear to be ignorant. But chances are, if they ask the question, the teacher or other people might have the same question! It's possible to fellowship in shared ignorance and stimulate one another to find the answer. Your ignorance in a sense is the foundation of your understanding and learning. Look for things you are ignorant about, and find the answers to fill the holes in your knowledge. The disciples didn't know the truth and seldom bothered to ask about it. They sat blindly in their ignorance, afraid to ask questions.

1. Christ's desire to share with the disciples

Jesus wanted the disciples to have answers to their questions. He wanted to share His heart with them. If they had said, "Lord, tell us about Your anguish over the cross. We want to identify with You and pray alongside You. We want to care for You," Jesus probably would have shared volumes of fantastic things with them. But in their selfishness, they couldn't see beyond their own problems. Jesus wanted to tell them that He didn't like the cross and that He looked beyond the cross to the joy that would be His (Heb. 12:2). The joy wasn't in the cross itself, but in what was accomplished on the cross.

Rather than care for Himself, Jesus accepted the disciples' indifference toward Him and tried to comfort them. His attempt to bring joy to the disciples perhaps helped Him to look past the nails, the thorns, the spear, and the cross to the victory in the coming of the Spirit. Christ would have wanted to look past Calvary as much as possible because it anguished Him. He sweat great drops of blood when He contemplated His death (Luke 22:44).

2. Christ's approach to comforting the disciples

In verses 16-24, you will notice that Christ is more concerned with the disciples' sorrow than their ignorance. He didn't try to deal with them theologically. He dealt with them in love and comfort. He could wait until His resurrection to deal with their ignorance; it was their sorrow that needed immediate attention. Isn't that a beautiful insight into how much He loved them? That's the essence of His care and love, and that's how He deals with us.

I believe Jesus' main concern is to comfort us before He gives us a theological education. He wants us to know peace, joy, and comfort. He didn't worry about the disciples' theological understanding in John 16 because He knew they would soon be theologians without parallel. He knew that ten days after He ascended, on the Day of Pentecost, the disciples would become walking scholars. Because that was inevitable in time, Christ was concerned more about the disciples' sorrow. He is a loving Savior, not an indifferent God. Many people portray God as indifferent and uncaring, but He is concerned with the comfort and care of His beloved children.

In verse 19, we see that Christ reads the disciples' minds like a billboard. In John 2:24-25 we see that Jesus could read what was in the heart of a man. From our perspective, there are positives and negatives about that ability. I'm glad the Lord can read my mind. Peter once said to Christ, "Lord, thou knowest all things; thou knowest that I love thee" (John 21:27). Aren't you glad the Lord knows you love Him even when you don't act like it? But I'm sure there are times when we may wish the Lord couldn't read our minds. In John 16:19, the Lord knows the disciples are struggling with what He had said in verses 17-18.

C. The Surprise (v. 19)

"Now Jesus knew that they were desirous to ask him, and said unto them, Do ye inquire among yourselves of what I said, A little while, and ye shall not see me; and again, a little while, and ye shall see me?"

The Lord knew the disciples were puzzled, so He asked the question for them. He knew they couldn't figure out what He meant by the phrase "a little while." He asked, "Is what I said confusing you?" You can imagine how quickly the disciples jumped up when they heard that; Jesus had read their minds. Isn't it great to know that the Lord knows our problems before we ever articulate them? He knows exactly what we need before we say a word. In Isaiah 65:24, the Lord says, "Before they call, I will answer; and while they are yet speaking, I will hear." The disciples hadn't asked their question yet, and the Lord already had an answer for them. To comfort them, Christ shared an illustration with a tremendous spiritual principle.

III. THE PARABLE (vv. 20-22)

A. The Instruction (v. 20)

"Verily, verily, I say unto you, Ye shall weep and lament, but the world shall rejoice; and ye shall be sorrowful, but your sorrow shall be turned into joy."

1. The prediction

The use of the word *verily* twice indicates that Christ was making a critical, solemn statement. He made a great promise to the sorrowing disciples: Your sorrow is going to turn into joy. Notice that Jesus depicted the depth of their sorrow with the phrase "weep and lament." He did that so their future joy might look all the more beautiful. He painted a black backdrop and injected the statement about joy at the end of the verse: "Your sorrow shall be turned into joy."

2. The principle

   a) In relation to the disciples

   Christ was telling the disciples that the event causing
   their grief would be the same event that would bring
   them joy. He wasn't saying He would replace sorrowful events with happy ones. The point is, whatever
   brings you sorrow now will bring you joy later on (Ps.
   30:5). It's not a matter of saying, "Such-and-such was
   bad, and it caused me grief, so I'll put it in my grief
   box. That was good; I'll put it in my happy box." The
   Lord takes our sorrow over a particular event and
   turns it into joy. Whatever plunges you into grief will
   lift you into joy.

   What was it that was about to give the disciples great
   sorrow? The cross. But after Christ's death and resurrection, the cross became the source of their joy. Paul
   said, "God forbid that I should glory, except in the
   cross of our Lord Jesus Christ" (Gal. 6:14). Throughout the book of Acts, the apostles happily praised
   God and preached the message about the cross. Unbelievers may wonder how anyone could be happy
   over the crucifixion of his leader. What looks like a
   sorrowful event to them is a joyful event for
   Christians.

   b) In relation to us

   The disciples had to wait until after the cross for
   their sorrow to turn into joy. That's how God wants
   to work in our lives: He wants to take our sorrows
   and make them joys; it's not that He balances all the
   sad events in our lives with happy ones. In Romans
   8:28 Paul says, "All things work together for good to
   them that love God, to them who are the called according to his purpose." The Lord turns sorrow into
   joy, just as He turned water into wine (John 2:7-9).
   He didn't replace the water with wine. The disciples
   had their sorrow turned to joy when the Spirit came
   on the Day of Pentecost. The source of their grief,
   which was the cross, became the source of their
   greatest joy.

What Is the Source of Our Joy?

The cross is the source of our joy, not circumstances. If you concern yourself with circumstances, you will find problems. The cross was the foundation of the disciples' joy, and the same is true for us. In John 20:20, we read that the disciples were glad when they saw the risen Lord. When Jesus appears to two of the disciples on the road to Emmaus in Luke 24, they become happy. They felt their hearts burn within them as they walked with the resurrected Christ (v. 32). We see in the book of Acts that the people in the early church were a happy bunch. They were happy over the cross.

God wants to take the sorrow in your life and turn it to joy. If you never experienced sorrow and had only joy, the joy would be neutral. Trust that God wants to change your sorrows into joy—He will do so if you can wait long enough.

Sorrow comes into our lives mainly for two reasons. One reason is the testing of our faith. If you endure the test and become stronger as a result of it, that is cause for joy. We also experience sorrow when God chastises us. But God punishes us so that we won't disobey Him again, and that is cause for joy. In everything that happens in your life, try to find the glimmer of joy that's beginning to break from your sorrow. Even if you are in a disastrous situation, God can take that disaster and turn it into joy.

In 2 Corinthians 6:10 Paul says he is "sorrowful, yet always rejoicing." He had many problems. He had great heaviness in his heart (Rom. 9:2). But he also said, "Rejoice in the Lord always; and again I say, Rejoice" (Phil. 4:4). How can we be sorrowful and always rejoicing? We can rejoice because of the cross and because we know God will turn the water of sorrow into the wine of rejoicing. Jesus tells the disciples in John 15:11, "These things have I spoken unto you, that my joy might remain in you, and that your joy might be full." He said their sorrow would turn to joy, and it did. They were the happiest group of men on earth after the Spirit came on the Day of Pentecost.

B. The Illustration (v. 21)

1. Initial sorrow (v. 21*a*)

"A woman, when she is in travail [childbirth], hath sorrow, because her hour is come."

Experiencing pain and sorrow is a part of the curse from Eve's sin. She brought upon women the pain of childbirth (Gen. 3:16). When a woman is about to have a child, she has great pain. My wife once said she hoped I understood what she went through during childbirth; yet only mothers fully understand what it's like.

2. Inevitable joy (v. 21*b*)

"But as soon as she is delivered of the child, she remembereth no more the anguish, for the joy that a man is born into the world."

That illustration shows an event that started out in grief and anguish yet ended up in joy. The sorrow and pain of the mother is completely washed out when the baby is born. When you see that precious little life, you don't remember the anguish anymore.

Jesus was telling the disciples, "When I die and am no longer with you, you'll be lonely and experience sorrow. But trust Me that out of your sorrow will come the greatest possible joy." Ask any woman with children about her greatest joy, and she will most likely say the birth of her children. Jesus used the greatest example of human joy to illustrate that God can turn our sorrow to joy.

C. The Insurance (v. 22)

"And ye now, therefore, have sorrow; but I will see you again, and your heart shall rejoice, and your joy no man taketh from you."

1. The promise of joy

   The disciples were experiencing birth pains because they anticipated Christ's departure and their loneliness. But imagine how thrilled they were to hear that they would see Jesus again, and even more surprised when the Lord said, "Your joy no man taketh from you."

2. The permanence of joy

   The joy we have as a result of Christ's work on the cross is an eternal joy. Your life might fall apart, you might lose the joy that comes from your circumstances, and you might not be able to believe God can bring joy out of sadness; but the cross can be a constant source of joy for you. No man can ever undo the work of grace that God did in your life through the cross. Someone might put you in difficult circumstances or bring you grief, or you might bring sorrow upon yourself. But no matter what happens, no one can violate the perfect work Christ did on the cross in your behalf. The joy Christ promises the disciples in John 16 is the joy that would come from Calvary. No man can take from you the absolute security you have as a believer. The work on the cross cannot be reversed, and the joy from it is permanently ours.

   Since Christ is talking about a permanent joy, we know that the joy the disciples experience during the second "little while" in verse 16 has to go beyond the resurrection. It's an eternal joy that will never pass away. That's why Paul was able to rejoice always even in the midst of the sorrows in his life. He couldn't always understand every circumstance, but he believed that God could bring joy out of every circumstance. He didn't care about getting beaten up or put in jail; he was mature enough to see that joy could come from grief. I'm sure there were times when Paul failed to look for joy in a circumstance because he was discouraged. But the one joy no one could ever take from him was the joy he had in the cross. That's the source of every believer's joy.

IV. THE PROMISE (vv. 23-24)

A. Of Full Understanding (v. 23a)

"And in that day ye shall ask me nothing."

What day was Christ referring to? The day He spoke of in verse 22: the day the Spirit would come. That would be the day when their sorrow would turn to joy, and the Lord would come back to dwell within the disciples.

The word *day* can be used to refer to an era. For example, the biblical phrase "the day of the Lord" basically refers to a period of time. Frequently we use the word *day* to speak of an era when we say, "This is the day of science." So in that day or age of the Spirit, beginning at Pentecost, the disciples would no longer ask Jesus questions.

Why wouldn't the disciples ask the Lord anything? For one thing, Christ would no longer be physically present with them. Also, Christ told the disciples that when the Spirit came, He would teach them all things and remind them of what Christ said to them (John 14:26). The Spirit would lead them into all truth and make them scholars. Because of that, the disciples wouldn't need Christ around to answer their questions. But the Lord knew the disciples would still have needs. That's what He addresses next in John 16:23.

B. Of Provision (v. 23b)

"Verily, verily, I say unto you, Whatever ye shall ask the Father in my name, he will give it you."

Christ was saying, "You are about to enter into a new age. No longer will I be here to answer your questions and care for you. From now on, you will be able to pray to the Father in My name and receive your resources from Him." He says the same thing in John 14:13-14: "Whatever ye shall ask in my name, that will I do, that the Father may be glorified in the Son. If ye shall ask anything in my name, I will do it." In John 15:16 we read that whatever we ask of the Father in Christ's name, He will give it to us. We've seen Christ say that to the disciples several times already. Whatever we ask in the name of Jesus, God will give it to us.

What Does It Mean to Pray in Jesus' Name?

Can you just make a request to God, then say, "In Jesus' name I pray, amen"? Will that guarantee you'll get what you requested? No; to ask in Jesus' name means to ask for something in behalf of Christ. You are saying, "Father, I want that because Christ wants it." Saying that should help keep you from making any selfish prayer requests. We are to pray for what Jesus would want. In fact, the Bible doesn't discuss at length the need to pray for ourselves. We might ask God to give us wisdom or guidance, but we don't really need to ask Him for many things. Some people ask God for guidance, but God may be saying, "I'm trying to guide you; why don't you follow?" We need to pray for what we know to be Jesus' will, such as growing in godliness and studying God's Word. That's Christ's will for us, and God will answer such requests. We can ask the Father in behalf of Christ for the salvation of a person, because the Bible says the Lord is not willing that any should perish (2 Pet. 3:9).

C. Of a New Age (v. 24a)

"Hitherto have ye asked nothing in my name."

Christ was saying that up to that time, the disciples hadn't prayed in His name. They were about to enter into a new age in which they could do that. Some commentators believe Christ was rebuking the disciples for not asking for anything in His name. But that's not what He was doing; He was simply explaining to them the character of the new age.

D. Of Joy Through Answered Prayer (v. 24b)

"Ask, and ye shall receive, that your joy may be full."

There are three categories Christians can fit into in terms of joy: those who have no joy, those whose joy is found through the cross, and those who have full joy. How can we have full joy? Jesus gives the answer in John 16:24: "Hitherto have ye asked nothing in my name; ask, and ye shall receive, that your joy may be full." So how can we know full joy? By asking God for things and receiving them. We can know full joy through answered prayer.

Do you get excited when God answers your prayers? Scripture talks about joy in prayer. First Thessalonians 5:16 says, "Rejoice evermore." How? The next verse says, "Pray without ceasing." Philippians 4 says, "Rejoice in the Lord always; and again I say, Rejoice. . . . Be anxious for nothing, but in everything, by prayer and supplication with thanksgiving, let your requests be made known unto God" (vv. 4, 6). Full joy comes from answered prayer.

When you tap into God's resources and see God at work in your life, that's cause for joy! Christians who go around griping and being cynical do so because they haven't activated the power of God on their behalf. They aren't basking in a prayer-without-ceasing kind of life, allowing God to work in their lives in a way that brings joy. If you want joy, you'll find it on your knees in deep communion with God. Pray and talk to Him. It's joy just to be in His presence! And your cup of joy will overflow as you behold God's grace and love and see Him answer your prayers.

Conclusion

In responding to the disciples' sorrow, Jesus didn't tell them they would understand everything later on. He didn't discuss theology. Instead, He told them they were going to have joy—not just as a result of the cross but from constant communion with the Father. We can all receive joy as a result of Christ's work on the cross. We can even receive a certain extent of joy from circumstances. But full joy comes from praying without ceasing. In everything, we should make our requests known by prayer and supplication.

Everything Jesus says to the disciples in John 16:16-24 should have made them glad. He said that the separation between them would be brief and that their sorrow would turn to joy after the cross. He also said the joy they would receive would be permanent—no one could ever take it away from them. Finally, He said they could make their joy more full by staying in constant communion with God, asking and receiving things in His name.

Again, we can't help but see the beauty and magnificence of the person of Jesus Christ. What a Savior! He knew the cross was coming; He could already see with His mind's eye the nails tearing into His limbs, the thorns puncturing His brow, the spear into His internal organs, the jeers of the mocking people, and the spit and laughter of His killers. He could already feel the loneliness of being separated from God, and the pain of bearing every sin of mankind. But even in anticipation of all that, He wanted most of all to make the disciples happy. That tells me He really cares for us. In the midst of all that He must be doing to uphold the universe, He cares that we have joy. Right up to His death on the cross, Christ did everything to assure us full joy. He provided a glorious prayer fellowship with the Father, and He sent His Holy Spirit to live within us—all because He wants us to have joy. It must break the Lord's heart when a Christian becomes bitter or cynical and doesn't take hold of the joy he could have. God forgive us if we are not overwhelmed with the sweet joy that is ours because of the cross and with the way He can turn sorrow into joy.

Focusing on the Facts

1. What is one of the greatest ways to comfort a person in sorrow (see p. 42)?
2. What does the phrase "a little while" refer to in John 7:33; 12:35; and 13:33 (see pp. 43-44)?
3. How do we know that the second "little while" in John 16:16 does not refer to the second coming or the resurrection (see pp. 44-45)?
4. When Jesus told the disciples they would see Him again after He departed, what was He talking about (see p. 46)?
5. What evidence in John 14:16-18 and Matthew 28:20 supports the answer in the previous question (see pp. 46-47)?
6. When was Christ's promise that the disciples would see Him again fulfilled (see p. 47)?
7. Why were the disciples silent in John 16:18? Should we follow their example in similar situations? Explain your answer (see p. 49).
8. What might Christ's attempt to bring joy to His disciples have helped Him to do (see p. 50)?
9. What is Christ most concerned about in relation to His disciples in John 16:16-24, and why (see p. 50)?

10. How did the Lord surprise the disciples in John 16:19 (see p. 51)?
11. Our sorrow will be _____ into joy, not _____ by joy (see p. 52).
12. What is the source of our joy? What are two main reasons for sorrow coming into our lives (see p. 53)?
13. What is Christ trying to explain through the illustration about childbirth in John 16:21 (see p. 54)?
14. According to John 16:22, what is true about the joy we have because of the cross (see p. 55)?
15. What did Christ promise to the disciples in John 16:23-24 (see pp. 56-57)?
16. Explain how joy and prayer are related (see p. 58).

Pondering the Principles

1. When the disciples were sorrowful, Jesus comforted them. He didn't try to clear up their misunderstanding with theological explanations. That is a good example for you when you minister to someone who is brokenhearted or depressed. Such a person needs a listening ear before you give him counsel. Work on being a sympathetic listener in addition to being a biblically sound counselor.

2. The best way to see the joy that comes from answered prayer is to keep a record of your prayer requests. As time goes along and you see prayers answered, you will notice how God is working in your life. To make your own prayer log, write down your daily prayer requests and the date you made the requests. Then, whenever a specific request is answered, put a check mark by it. Not only does a prayer log make you more aware of God's answers to your prayers, it also serves as a constant reminder of what God has done for you in the past. That can be a source of comfort when the future looks uncertain.

4

Peace: A By-Product of Faith, Hope, and Love—Part 1

Outline

Introduction
A. The Search
B. The Solution

Lesson
I. Love (vv. 25-27)
   A. The Promise of Understanding (v. 25)
      1. The age of speaking in proverbs
         a) The communication of veiled statements
         b) The category of veiled statements
         c) The comprehension of veiled statements
      2. The age of speaking plainly
         a) The Teacher who clarifies spiritual truth
         b) The transition in clarifying spiritual truth
            (1) The veiled glory of the Old Covenant
            (2) The unveiled glory of the New Covenant
   B. The Privilege in Prayer (v. 26)
      1. The details about our access to God (v. 26a)
      2. The degree of our access to God (v. 26b)
   C. The Proclamation of Love (v. 27)
      1. Explaining God's love
      2. Emulating God's love
      3. Examining God's love
      4. Experiencing God's love

Introduction

In John 16:25-33, Jesus Christ wraps up His conversation with His disciples the night before His death. These verses summarize everything He has said from John 13 onward. The theme of this portion of Scripture is faith, hope, love, and the result of those things, which is peace.

A. The Search

We live in a bleak world; I'm sure it's obvious to you the sad state our world is in. If anything is true, it's that men today are desperate for love, something to believe in, and something to hope for. People recognize that a man must be worth something to someone; that's what love is. It's a value system that sets a certain worth on an individual. And people today want to know they are valuable. They want to know they mean something, not that they are part of some cosmic machine. They want love.

We live in a world where you can't put your faith in anything. People want something to hope for. They say there has to be a better world somewhere, where inequalities become equal, injustice becomes justice, wrongs are made right, and bad is turned into good. There is a new world coming; it will be created by Jesus Christ, and it's called the kingdom of God. There is something to hope for, but the world doesn't know that. The people in our world are despairing because they can't find what they are looking for. Jesus addresses that matter in John 16.

B. The Solution

Man exists because God wanted him to. Since God wanted man to be, He has wonderful things in store for all mankind. The things that man is looking for—faith, hope, and love—are exactly what Jesus can give him. First Corinthians 13:13 says, "Now abideth faith, hope, love, these three; but the greatest of these is love." Those three things come from having a relationship with Jesus Christ. He gives man what he needs most. Man cannot exist without faith, hope, and love, and those are the things Jesus talks about in John 16:25-33.

A superficial reading of John 16:25-33 might not reveal that Jesus is talking about those things, but a careful study of the discourse between Jesus and the disciples makes them become more apparent. Now faith, hope, and love are the three cardinal virtues of salvation. They summarize the Lord's discourse in John 13-16. Nothing more is said about Judaism; rather, Christ talks about the new age and the dispensation of the Holy Spirit. He deals with the Christian's position before God. Judaism is fading away from the scene. In John 16:25-33, the Lord offers to His disciples—and to every man who comes to Him—faith, hope, and love, the three things that make existence meaningful.

Lesson

I. LOVE (vv. 25-27)

A. The Promise of Understanding (v. 25)

"These things have I spoken unto you in proverbs; but the time cometh when I shall no more speak unto you in proverbs, but I shall show you plainly of the Father."

1. The age of speaking in proverbs

a) The communication of veiled statements

The Greek word translated "proverb" is *paroimias*. There are two words in the New Testament that were used to refer to the veiled statements of Jesus: *parabalas*, which is translated "parable," and *paroimia*, which is translated "proverb." However, the latter translation may not be the best English translation of John 16:25, as we usually think of a proverb as a clever, short saying. But the Greek word *paroimia* means "a veiled, pointed statement." The Hebrew equivalent of that word speaks of a statement full of meaning. The statement is like an iceberg that is largely hidden under the water's surface.

Jesus frequently spoke in that manner and in so doing kept unbelievers from understanding what He was saying. Those who in a worldly sense were wise and prudent didn't understand Jesus. Even the disciples were limited in their understanding. They understood only the basics of what the Lord said, and that's all that Jesus wanted. He left the deeper meanings for later when the Holy Spirit would give believers special insight.

Jesus left a wealth of information that would require the later teaching of the Holy Spirit. By sovereign design, He spoke in veiled statements that would limit people's ability to understand them. One example of such a statement appears in John 2:19, where Jesus says, "Destroy this temple, and in three days I will raise it up." The people who heard that must have scratched their heads and wondered how He could possibly do that. But they didn't realize He was talking about His body until He rose from the grave. The truth He states in John 2:19 unfolds later on. The disciples understood a little of what Christ said at the time, but the world understood none of it.

Some other veiled statements Christ made were, "I am the light of the world" (John 8:12) and, "I am the bread of life" (John 6:35). In John 6:53-57 He talks about eating His flesh and drinking His blood. The Jewish religious leaders didn't understand what He meant. They probably thought, *There is not enough of you physically for everyone in town, let alone the world!* The Jewish leaders didn't entirely understand Jesus when He said, "Before Abraham was, I am" (John 8:58). Whenever the Lord spoke in veiled statements, enough of it was understood to make it meaningful, yet a rich truth always remained hidden for the Holy Spirit to reveal later on. Christ gave enough information to leave a man without excuse for rejecting Him, but there was enough left unsaid for the Spirit of God to spend this whole age of grace unfolding it for us.

b) The category of veiled statements

When Jesus said, "These things have I spoken unto you in proverbs," what things was He referring to? It's possible He was making a reference to the content of His veiled statements in general. But more specifically, the Lord was referring to the statements He made about the Father, as evidenced by the phrase "of the Father" at the end of verse 25. He had just talked to the disciples about His coming from God and going back to God, all in veiled statements. In fact, Christ had talked about coming and going to the Father throughout the gospel of John. He had spoken in contexts that made it hard for the disciples to figure out exactly what He was saying. So now He in effect says, "I've been speaking to you in veiled statements about My relationship to the Father." The divine origin of Christ and His return to His divine place was a big mystery.

Not only did Christ design His statements to be veiled, but He also knew the disciples wouldn't yet understand certain truths. In John 16:12 He tells them, "I have yet many things to say unto you, but ye cannot bear them now." The disciples were doing well to see the tops of the icebergs—to understand the basics of what Christ was saying. They were spiritually ignorant and unable to understand certain things prior to Christ's death. That's not their fault, though, because they didn't yet have within them the resident Holy Spirit, who would teach them.

Some of the statements that confused the disciples don't confuse us. When we read that Jesus came from God and went back to Him, we understand that. When the Lord spoke to the disciples, His statements were veiled not only by His own design but also by their ignorance. Yet He promises the disciples in John 16:13, "The Spirit of truth . . . will guide you into all truth; for he shall not speak of himself, but whatever he shall hear, that shall he speak." In John 14:26 Jesus says, "The Holy Spirit . . . shall teach you all things, and bring all things to your remembrance, whatever I have said unto you." So until Christ died, rose again, and the Spirit came, the disciples would not fully understand His teaching about His relationship to the Father. When the Spirit came, He would speak to them plainly about the Father, not in veiled statements.

c) The comprehension of veiled statements

Christ says in John 16:25 that "the time cometh when I shall no more speak to you in proverbs." That refers to the same time spoken of in the phrases "in that day" (v. 23) and "at that day" (v. 26): the Day of Pentecost, when the Spirit of God would come and permanently indwell the disciples and all other believers. From the coming of the Holy Spirit on the Day of Pentecost—which was about fifty days after Christ died—on up to now and throughout the age of grace, the Spirit of God will dwell in all believers. So in John 16:25, Jesus is saying that when the Spirit came they would understand the mysteries in the statements He made.

That the truths Christ taught became clear and easy to understand as a result of the Spirit's teaching is evident in the writings of Paul, James, Peter, and all the other New Testament writers. They didn't write in parables. The only book that has mysteries in it is Revelation, and that's because it talks about future events. The book of Revelation is to us what Christ's veiled statements were to the disciples. But all the epistles are designed to unfold Christ's teachings to us. They were written to unveil the mysteries and teach the truth plainly. So from the time the Spirit of God came and afterward, the disciples would understand Christ's veiled statements. In fact, Jesus says in John 16:23, "In that day ye shall ask me nothing." Their questions would be answered in the new age.

It's easy for us to think of the disciples as dimwitted. We read what Christ taught them, think it's easy to understand, and say that the disciples should have understood it better. But remember that within us lives the Holy Spirit of God. Without the Spirit, we would be worse off than the disciples. At least they had Christ with them to answer their questions. First Corinthians 2:9 says, "It is written, Eye hath not seen, nor ear heard, neither have entered into the heart of man, the things which God hath prepared for them that love him." Our human senses and understanding are not capable of helping us to understand the veiled truths in Scripture.

2. The age of speaking plainly

   a) The Teacher who clarifies spiritual truth

   First Corinthians 2:10 tells us that spiritual truths are revealed to us by God's Spirit. The only reason we understand anything in Scripture is that the Holy Spirit is our teacher. Whenever a person tells me he doesn't know if the Holy Spirit is in him, I ask him, "Do you understand the Bible?" If the answer is yes, it's because the Holy Spirit lives within him. It is the Spirit who knows the deep things of God and teaches them to us (1 Cor. 2:10-11). Verses 12-14 say, "Now we have received, not the spirit of the world, but the Spirit who is of God; that we might know the things that are freely given to us of God. Which things also we speak, not in the words which man's wisdom teacheth, but which the Holy Spirit teacheth, comparing spiritual things with spiritual. But the natural man receiveth not the things of the Spirit of God . . . because they are spiritually discerned."

   You know about God only because the Spirit of God is your teacher. He is the only one who knows the mind of God, and He reveals the deep things of God to you and me. The spiritual truths we know are understood with the help of the Spirit. Sometimes He teaches us directly and other times we learn from Him through other people. But it's all the Spirit's teaching.

   b) The transition in clarifying spiritual truth

   There are a couple of points I'd like to highlight in 2 Corinthians 3. There we read that we have trust "through Christ toward God; not that we are sufficient of ourselves to think anything as of ourselves, but our sufficiency is of God, who also hath made us able ministers of the new testament, not of the letter, but of the spirit; for the letter killeth, but the Spirit giveth life" (vv. 4-6).

(1) The veiled glory of the Old Covenant

The phrase "the letter" in verse 6 refers to Old Testament law. Did you know that the law kills because we can't keep it? When you break the law, the result is death.

Verse 7 calls the law "the ministration of death." It was "written and engraved in stones, was glorious, so that the children of Israel could not steadfastly behold the face of Moses for the glory of his countenance, which glory was to be done away" (v. 7). Paul then asked, "How shall not the ministration of the Spirit be more glorious?" (v. 8). Paul was saying, "If the Old Covenant was good enough to put a glow on Moses' face and bring glory to God, how much more glory the New Covenant will bring!" Verse 9 says, "If the ministration of condemnation be glory, much more doth the ministration of righteousness exceed in glory." The law condemns us. The only way you can be saved by God's law is to keep all of it. Since you can't do that, the law can only condemn you. If a law that condemns is glorious, how much more glorious is a New Testament that can give righteousness!

In verse 10 we read, "Even that which was made glorious had no glory in this respect, by reason of the glory that excelleth." When you compare the Old Covenant to the New, the Old looks less glorious. Verses 11 and 12 say, "If that which is done away [i.e., the Old Covenant] was glorious, much more that which remaineth is glorious. Seeing, then, that we have such hope, we use great plainness of speech." Veiled statements, pictures, and types of things to come in the Old Testament are now understood. Pictures and prophecies regarding the Messiah no longer need to be unscrambled. That's why Paul says in verse 12, "We use great plainness of speech."

The glory of the New Covenant was not like the temporary glory that Moses had on his face.

Verse 13 says Moses "put a veil over his face, that the children of Israel could not steadfastly look to the end of that which is abolished." After Moses came down from Mount Sinai with the tablets of the law, he put a veil over his face to hide the glory because it was fading away. According to verse 14, the Old Testament had a veiled glory. The Israelites didn't understand its parables, types, and pictures. The Old Covenant did not have plainness of speech.

(2) The unveiled glory of the New Covenant

When Jesus appeared to the disciples on the road to Emmaus, He told them that if they had really known the Old Testament, they would have understood the events surrounding the cross and the promise of the resurrection (Luke 24:25-26). The disciples didn't understand the Old Testament Scriptures. The Jewish religious leaders had even less of an understanding. That's why Paul says in 2 Corinthians 3:14, "Their minds were blinded; for until this day remaineth the same veil untaken away in the reading of the old testament; which veil is done away in Christ." But two thousand years after Christ took away the veil, many Jewish people still have that veil on (v. 15). Verse 16 says, "Nevertheless when [an individual] shall turn to the Lord, the veil shall be taken away."

Verses 17-18 close by saying, "Now the Lord is that Spirit; and where the Spirit of the Lord is, there is liberty. But we all, with unveiled face [i.e., with clear understanding of the New Testament] beholding as in a mirror the glory of the Lord, are changed into the same image from glory to glory, even as by the Spirit of the Lord." As we gaze into the unclouded glory of Christ in the New Testament, the Spirit progressively changes us into the Lord's image. That's what Christianity is: becoming like Christ. The only way to do that is to gaze into His unveiled glory while the Spirit changes you.

The Old Testament is filled with veiled statements, parables, types, and prophecies. The present age of grace is marked by plainness of speech. Things are clearer to us because the indwelling Spirit is our teacher. There was a tremendous change when the Spirit came; a whole new age was born. The disciples lived in the veiled age. They heard what Christ said in the context of a legalistic society. They couldn't decipher everything He said. But with the coming of the Spirit, everything became clear to them because the Spirit became their teacher. That's what Jesus means when He says in John 16:25, "These things have I spoken unto you in proverbs; but the time cometh when I shall no more speak unto you in proverbs, but I shall show you plainly of the Father." Isn't that a tremendous promise?

As Christians, we may not know all the doctrines of the Bible, but we definitely know the Father. Even a spiritual babe—a new Christian—knows Him. In 1 John 2:13 we read, "I write unto you, little children, because ye have known the Father." A baby doesn't understand much, but he knows his mom and dad. A new Christian may not know much, but he knows the Father. The first thing a new believer learns is that God loves him and cares for him. Christ promises in John 16 that in the new age we would know the Father. We would have no questions about Him. We would also understand Christ's relationship to the Father and the redemptive plan that God designed for mankind, which involves both Christ and the Holy Spirit. We know the Father, Christ, and the Spirit—the Trinity. God, Christ, and the Spirit are three in one, according to God's Word. We may not completely understand that, but we believe it.

B. The Privilege in Prayer (v. 26)

"At that day ye shall ask in my name, and I say not unto you, that I will pray the Father for you."

70

First Jesus said we will be able to pray to the Father in His name, then He said, "I say not unto you, that I will pray the Father for you." Was He saying that He will never pray for us? That would contradict Romans 8:34, which says that Christ sits at the right hand of God interceding for us. Let's find out what Christ was saying by examining the verse.

1. The details about our access to God (v. 26a)

"At that day ye shall ask in my name."

With the coming of the Spirit, the disciples would be able to do what they had never done before: go directly to the Father in the name of Jesus. In John 16:23-24 Christ tells them, "Whatever ye shall ask the Father in my name, he will give it you. Hitherto have ye asked nothing in my name; ask, and ye shall receive, that your joy may be full." A new age was coming, and the disciples would be able to go directly to the Father with their requests, provided their requests were in Jesus' name. To pray in Jesus' name means to pray for what He would want. You can't just pray for anything you want. You need to say, "Father, I come because Jesus sent me, and I'm asking You to do this for His sake." You are to ask for what is consistent with Christ's will. When you do that, God will give what you ask for.

The Father loves the Son. Because of that, anyone who comes to the Father in the Son's name is going to get what he asks for. If someone came to me and asked for something my son wanted, as long as it's right and good, I would grant the request. I would also grant it quickly because of my love for my son. The same is true of God. He answers prayer but more so when He knows we are sent by His Son, whom He loves with an infinite love. So prayer is the power to move God's hand. It is a joy and involves going directly into God's presence.

We live in a new age where the Spirit of God dwells in us when we put our faith and love in Jesus Christ. And through prayer, we have immediate access to God. With that in mind, let's examine the seemingly confusing statement at the end of John 16:26.

2. The degree of our access to God (v. 26*b*)

"I say not unto you, that I will pray the Father for you."

Jesus wasn't saying He wouldn't pray for us; He was saying, "You won't need Me to pray to God for you. You're able to go directly to the Father. You don't need to have Me beg to God on your behalf; just go to Him in My name. You belong to Me, and the Father loves Me so much that whatever you ask in My name, for My sake He will do it for you." When we go into God's presence, we are received just as God would receive His own Son. We have instant, total access to God's divine presence.

Jesus doesn't need to pray for us. I can pray for certain things in my own life. But there are times when, according to Romans 8:34, Christ makes intercession for us. Romans 8:26 tells us how: through the Spirit of Christ within us. Paul wrote, "The Spirit . . . helpeth our infirmity; for we know not what we should pray for as we ought; but the Spirit himself maketh intercession for us with groanings which cannot be uttered." Do you know when Christ intercedes for us? When we don't know how to pray. We can go directly to God regarding our own needs, anxiety, requests, and desires. But when we don't know how to pray or what to pray for, Christ helps us. He takes care of the things we cannot even think of.

First John 2 tells us of another way He intercedes on our behalf: "If any man sin, we have an advocate with the Father, Jesus Christ the righteous" (v. 1). Christ intercedes for us when we sin, and asks the Father to forgive us, for He is "the propitiation for our sins" (1 John 2:2). So, Jesus takes care of the things we can't. Romans 8:28 says, "All things work together for good to them that love God, to them who are the called according to his purpose." That's because of the constant intercessory ministry of the Spirit of Christ on our behalf.

C. The Proclamation of Love (v. 27)

"The Father himself loveth you, because ye have loved me, and have believed that I came out from God."

It's fabulous to know that we can go immediately into God's presence. We don't have to pray as if God were behind a wall that needs to be smashed down. We can come to Him with our requests, and Jesus will pray for the things we don't know how to pray for, as well as intercede on behalf of our sins. Why is God willing to do that? We don't deserve such a privilege. What right do we have to expect God to allow us into His presence and have His Son intercede for us? The answer is in John 16:27: "The Father himself loveth you."

1. Explaining God's love

God allows us into His presence because He loves us. And why does He love us? Christ said, "Because ye have loved me, and have believed that I came out from God" (John 16:27). When you love Christ, God loves you with a unique kind of love. That love prompts bounty, blessing, and answered prayer on your behalf.

God loves you. You're worth something. That's the basis of human existence. If God didn't love you, then life would be a sick joke. But God does love you. Imagine —the God of the universe loves you! Doesn't that give you a sense of worth? You are so highly valued that Christ came to earth to die for you. That's how much God loves you.

How Much Does God Love You?

There's a very famous Greek word translated "love" in the Bible—*agape*. It is used to refer to divine love. But that's not the word used in John 16:27; Christ used *philei*, which means "really likes." God not only loves you with an overall love but also likes you. *Philei* is a deep affection, a familial love.

In the Greek text, *philei* is in the present tense, which communicates that God's deep affection for you is continual. He loves the whole world in a divine sense (John 3:16), but He has a deep, fatherly affection for those who love Jesus. That's why He hears and answers their prayers. They're part of His family; He cares for them. I like the fact that

73

God loves everyone but has an intimate love for those who love Jesus. It is because of God's universal divine love that He sent Christ to save us. I'm happy about His tender, fatherly affection for me because that makes Him want to give me what I ask for in Jesus' name. You can't be a Christian and understand God's love and deep affection without having a tremendous sense of worth.

You're the highest prize God ever claimed in the universe. When the angels fell, He never redeemed them. When man fell, He set everything in motion in the universe to redeem him—all because He loves us.

Some Christians think of God as being constantly after us with a whip. They say to their children, "Don't do that or God won't like you." It's wrong to say that. If you're a Christian, God likes you. Many Christians beat themselves down with persecution complexes and feelings of inadequacy. They think no one likes them. But God does. He has a deep, warm, tender fatherly affection for you. If you love Jesus and believe that He came from the Father—if you believe redemption is available through Christ—God has a warm, intimate love for you. Even though God knows we are unfaithful, sinful, and sour, He still loves us. He loves us with a constant affection.

2. Emulating God's love

One question comes to my mind when I think about God's tender affection for all Christians despite our faults: Do we love one another with the same kind of love, even though we know each others' faults? Most of us don't. Many of us would rather elevate ourselves above God and choose whom we desire to love. But as Jesus twice said to His disciples, "The servant is not greater than his lord" (John 13:16; 15:20). Jesus washed Judas's feet even when He knew Judas would betray Him. Instead of judging others, we ought to make our salvation visible by loving everyone in the Body of Christ. We ought to have the same gentle affection God has toward us.

3. Examining God's love

God likes us a lot. He's a Father to us. That's why when a Christian prays, he doesn't come to God in fear (Rom. 8:15). When we pray, we don't say, "God, I'm coming into your presence. Don't hit me; wait until you hear what I have to say." Rather, we say, "Abba, Father" (Rom. 8:15). The word *abba* means "daddy." It's a term of intimacy. When we go into God's presence, we can go to Him in complete confidence. We can say, "*Abba*, Father, here's my need," and bare our hearts before Him.

It's hard to explain God's love to those who don't know Christ. In the midst of a loveless world that exists on loveless lives, words, sex, and homes, God has real love to offer—not just divine love but a tender, warm affection that gives value to the soul. Sadly, some people aren't willing to value others. That proves we are infinitely less holy than God is. He can see in every one of us value enough for Him to die on the cross. When you sense His love and love Him in return, you will sense fulfillment. You will know why you live and what it means to be alive.

4. Experiencing God's love

How do we experience God's tender love? First, He proved His love toward us in that "while we were still sinners, Christ died for us" (Rom. 5:8). All you need to do is love Jesus Christ, believe He came from God, accept His death on the cross, and you'll experience God's love. If a man is not loved, he is worthless. Love gives value to man. One who believes in and knows God makes sense out of life because he is loved. He has the chief clue to the meaning of existence, which is human value. You matter to God. You're not just a piece of cosmic machinery. You're a beloved individual whom God loves in a vast, divine way and in a deep, affectionate way.

In John 14:21 Jesus says, "He that hath my commandments, and keepeth them, he it is that loveth me; and he that loveth me shall be loved of my Father." You show your love to Christ by obeying His commands, and God loves those who love Jesus. In verse 23 our Lord says, "If a man love me, he will keep my words; and my Father will love him." Every believer is in the same love relationship with God and Christ. We can bask in Their love.

We all want to be loved. We know we are lacking as persons if we are unloved. We are conscious of our guilt, loneliness, and despair. And God, who is loving, alleviates our problem by loving us. He expressed His love to us by a supreme sacrifice. He asks only one thing from us—to love Him back. How? By loving His Son and obeying His commands. When we do that, God shows us a warm, tender affection.

God created you so He could love you. When you love Him and He loves you in return, your existence has meaning. Apart from that love you have no meaning. Everyone needs to know the truth Paul states in Ephesians 1:6: in Christ, we are beloved of God.

Focusing on the Facts

1. What three things are people looking for today? Where can they find them (see p. 62)?
2. Christ frequently spoke in proverbs (Gk., *paroimia*). What does *paroimia* mean (see p. 63)?
3. Did people understand Christ's proverbs? Explain (see pp. 63-64).
4. What specific category of proverbs was Christ talking about in John 16:25 (see pp. 64-65)?
5. What did Christ mean when He told the disciples, "The time cometh when I shall no more speak to you in proverbs" (John 16:25; see p. 66)?
6. What does 1 Corinthians 2:10 tell us regarding spiritual truths (see p. 67)?
7. Explain what 2 Corinthians 3:17-18 says (see p. 69).
8. Through prayer, we have immediate _____ to _____ (see p. 71).
9. Explain what Jesus meant by saying, "I say not unto you, that I will pray the Father for you" (John 16:26; see pp. 71-72).
10. When does Christ intercede in prayer for us? How else does He intercede for us (see p. 72)?

11. Why does God allow us into His presence? Explain (John 16:27; see p. 73).
12. How did God show that He highly values us (see p. 73)?
13. God loves the whole world in a divine sense. What kind of love does He have for those who are His own (see p. 73-74)?
14. What Scripture indicates we are to love all Christians with the same love God shows them (see p. 74)?
15. How can a person experience God's love (see pp. 75-76)?

Pondering the Principles

1. First Corinthians 2:9 says we cannot humanly understand the truths in the Bible. Read verses 10-14. How are we enabled to understand scriptural truths (v. 10)? To whom is full knowledge of God limited (v. 11)? According to verse 14, why can't the natural man (i.e., an unbeliever) understand the things of God? Memorize verse 12, and let it be a constant reminder to you that through the Holy Spirit you can know truth and develop a deep love and understanding of the Bible.

2. In John 16:26 we learn that we have direct access to the Father through prayer. From Romans 8:26, 34 we learn that Christ will intercede for us when we need His help. What do those truths tell you about how much God wants to communicate with you and help you? Are you as zealous to pray to God as He is to listen to your prayers? Pray to Him about what's on your heart right now.

3. According to John 16:27, God has a special love for those who love and believe in Christ. He loves them with a deep, tender affection. What are some of the ways God has expressed His love for you? Reflect on your answer and determine how you can express greater love toward other Christians.

5

Peace: A By-Product of Faith, Hope, and Love—Part 2

Outline

Introduction
A. The Plight of Mankind
B. The Provision for Mankind

Review
I. Love (vv. 25-27)
  A. The Promise of Understanding (v. 25)
  B. The Privilege in Prayer (v. 26)
  C. The Proclamation of Love (v. 27)
    1. Explaining God's love
    2. Emulating God's love
    3. Examining God's love
    4. Experiencing God's love

Lesson
II. Faith (vv. 28-32)
  A. A Commentary on Faith
  B. A Cornerstone for Faith
    1. Believing in Christ's deity
    2. Believing in Christ's redemptive work
  C. A Call for Faith
    1. The announcement from Christ
      a) A clear presentation of the truth about Himself
        (1) The truth rejected
        (2) The truth proved
      b) A clear presentation of the truth of the gospel
    2. The apprehension by the disciples

Introduction

In John 16:25-33, Jesus talks about faith, hope, and love—that which brings inner peace to man. Man is missing those three ingredients in his soul. Everyone desires to love and be loved. People want something to believe in and something to hope for. Apart from love, faith, and hope, man has no reason to exist. Life becomes a meaningless treadmill. It is the plight of twentieth-century man to search for those three realities.

A. The Plight of Mankind

In a book entitled *Despair: A Moment or Way of Life* (Downer's Grove, Ill.: InterVarsity Press, 1971), Stephen Evans wrote that twentieth-century man is unique because of his ability to wipe out life. Death's imminence is real because the entire population of the world can be wiped out by nuclear bombs, germ warfare, chemical warfare, and pollution. And the greatest horror that every man lives with is the fear of his own death. He isn't bothered so much by the fact that everyone must die as he is that he must die. Every man fears the inevitability of death. Though twentieth-century man is unique in many ways, he is not unique in his fear of death. That fear has haunted all men.

What makes death even more fearful is that it is a one-time event and must be faced alone. Whether you die in a hospital surrounded by relatives or in a nuclear holocaust with the whole human race, death must be faced personally.

80

Since modern man has eliminated God from his life, he faces death without even God. By eliminating God, man also eliminates hope, for who then really loves him? Whom can he believe in for his eternal destiny? What can he hope for beyond this world? Without God, there is no hope beyond death. A man without answers to those questions will never have peace in his heart.

B. The Provision for Mankind

Jesus offers faith, hope, and love to every man. The beauty of the gospel message is that Christ made those three things accessible to you and me. From them we can have peace. In 1 Corinthians 13:13 the apostle Paul says, "Now abideth faith, hope, love, these three; but the greatest of these is love." It is exactly those three things Christ speaks of in John 16:25-33. He offers to every man a divine love, someone and something to believe in, and a hope that is steadfast and eternal. When a man has all that, he has peace.

Review

I. LOVE (vv. 25-27; see pp. 63-76)

A. The Promise of Understanding (v. 25; see pp. 63-70)

"These things have I spoken unto you in proverbs; but the time cometh when I shall no more speak unto you in proverbs, but I shall show you plainly of the Father."

Jesus frequently spoke to the disciples in veiled statements that couldn't be completely understood. But the time was coming when the Holy Spirit would dwell in them permanently. From that time on, the Lord would speak to them clearly about God.

B. The Privilege in Prayer (v. 26; see pp. 70-72)

"At that day ye shall ask in my name, and I say not unto you, that I will pray the Father for you."

From the day the Spirit begins indwelling a believer, he has immediate access into God's presence. We don't need to ask Jesus to go to God for us. We can pray directly to God in the name of Jesus Christ.

C. The Proclamation of Love (v. 27; see pp. 72-76)

"For the Father himself loveth you, because ye have loved me, and have believed that I came out from God."

We can go directly to God with our prayer requests because He loves us. Now God loves everyone with a universal love —the *agape* love spoken of in John 3:16. But the Greek word translated "love" in John 16:27 is *philei*, which refers to an intimate, affectionate love. God loves you as a member of His family. He has a general, divine love for all men, but He also has an intimate, familial affection for those who love Jesus Christ.

1. Explaining God's love (see pp. 73-74)

God hears and answers your prayers directly because of His affectionate love for you. When a man discovers that the infinite God of the universe loves him, he realizes there is a reason for his existence. The mysteries of the universe become logical, and he sees that God created everything to display His glory. When a man views God's glory and turns to God, the Lord will express His love in return.

Jesus says in John 16:27 that those who love Christ are loved by the Father with a warm, caring kind of love that is different from the general, divine love of God that encompasses every man. To be loved by God is the pinnacle of value. When you love something, you assign value to it. God has valued you to the degree that He not only loves you with a divine, sweeping love but also with a warm, familial affection. That's how valuable you are to Him! Knowing that is the pinnacle of existence. It's amazing to think that the God of the universe cares about us, let alone has an affectionate love for us! God is not a cosmic, indifferent power; He is a personal, loving Father who gives to man an infinite and eternal value by loving man with an infinite and eternal love.

And He shows us that love in spite of our sinfulness and selfishness! God loves us with unconditional love.

2. Emulating God's love (see p. 74)

3. Examining God's love (see pp. 74-75)

4. Experiencing God's love (see pp. 75-76)

It's simple for you and me to know God's love. Jesus says in John 16:27 that God loves those who love Him and believe that Jesus came from God. When you love Christ and believe in His deity—that He came from God to accomplish a redemptive work that is sufficient for a man's salvation—then you will know God's love.

In John 14:21 Jesus says, "He that hath my commandments, and keepeth them, he it is that loveth me; and he that loveth me shall be loved of my Father." God will love those who love Christ, and you can tell if you love Christ by whether you obey His commandments or not. The faith of someone who says he loves Christ but lives as if he doesn't care about Christ's commandments can be questioned on the basis of John 14:21. A person's love for Christ becomes evident through obedience to Him, and obedience is the key to the entire Christian life. John 14:23 repeats verse 21: "If a man love me, he will keep my words; and my Father will love him." So if you believe in Christ and love Him, you will enter into an incredible, unique kind of love relationship with God.

Every man is loved by God; every man is valuable. But those who love Christ sense their worth because they enjoy an intimate love relationship with God. In Ephesians 2:6-7 Paul says that when we were saved, God "raised us up together, and made us sit together in heavenly places in Christ Jesus; that in the ages to come he might show the exceeding riches of his grace in his kindness toward us through Jesus Christ." God's kindness is displayed in a special way when He lifts us up as a result of our belonging to Christ. Earlier in verse 4 we read of God's rich mercy and great love toward believers. The tremendous, unsearchable riches of God's mercy and love lift us up to the place where we become the recipients of His kindness and blessings forever.

When a man loves Christ, who is God in human flesh and the sacrifice for mankind's sins, God responds to him with a gentle, caring love that is different from His universal love. In a human sense, the difference between God's affectionate love and universal love could be described as a person's intimate love for his family and his general love for those who are outside his family. God loves all men, yet has a special love for those who belong to Christ.

Happiness for Saddy

Some time ago when I had the opportunity to preach with others in some of the prisons in Mississippi, I met a young man who had disvalued himself tremendously all through his life. He never had a family; he didn't know who his mother or father were. He had lived in different orphanages and moved around a lot. Somehow he acquired the name Saddy. When we talked to him, he simply identified himself as Saddy, even though he had a last name. He was always sad, and he said there was no God. He said that no one loved him and that everything we preached was a lie. One young man on our evangelistic team spent forty-five minutes talking to him. After the talk, we saw Saddy smile from ear to ear, his face beaming. He came over to me, shook my hand, and said, "Thank you, thank you, thank you! I learned something today. I learned that God loves me and that you love me." I'll never forget those words. Saddy's life was transformed because now he knew he had value; he knew that God loved him.

It's no wonder that those who deny God's existence think life is meaningless. Once you rule out God, you rule out any thought that He loves you and thereby give yourself no reason for existing. To be loved is the crown of life. It's the chief clue to the meaning of existence. And when you know you're loved, you'll be able to love others. The Bible says to love your neighbor as yourself, but you can't value him correctly unless you have the right understanding of your worth; and to God, you have great value.

Lesson

II. FAITH (vv. 28-32)

A. A Commentary on Faith

Every person lives by faith. We operate on the principles of faith in our everyday activities. We believe in our house, our car, the roads, the restaurants, and canned food. We trust certain things; we put our faith in many things. There's a song with the words "I believe in music." Some people believe in music, but that's not a secure thing to believe in. An older song says, "I believe for ev'ry drop of rain that falls, a flower grows." If you could count every raindrop and every flower in the world, you would probably find that not to be true. Many people put their faith in the various religious systems of the world. Those who belong to Alcoholics Anonymous are told to believe in a higher power. Everyone believes in something. Most people believe in themselves.

Oliver Wendell Holmes, Sr., said that it is faith in something that makes life worth living. That's a vague statement. What is a man to bet his life on? He could believe in money, but that doesn't last. The paper we print dollar bills on doesn't mean a thing. What can we believe in? Poet G. A. Studdert-Kennedy wrote: "I bet my life on Christ—Christ Crucified."

B. A Cornerstone for Faith

What certainty can a person believe in? God's unending love. When you come to know God's love, you can place your faith in it. How do we know God loves us? By Christ's death on the cross. I believe God loves me, and I'm betting my eternal destiny on that. That's not a gamble because God proved His love for me by dying on the cross. If a father tells his son he loves him, and in an emergency situation loses his life to rescue his son, no one would have to argue with the boy about whether his father really loved him.

I know God loves me because He came into this world in human flesh and died on a cross for me. He bore my sins in His own body; He took the punishment that I deserved. That tells me that God loves me.

1. Believing in Christ's deity

According to John 16:27, we can know the Father's intimate love when we love Christ and believe that He came from God. The basis of our faith is that Christ came from God. I would never know that God loves me if He didn't show His love, and the greatest proof of it is in Christ's coming to earth. We can believe in God's love because He revealed it to us. We can't discover God's love on our own; He has to disclose it to us. We can see in the Old Testament that God did reveal His love to the people of that era. But His love became fully realized only when Christ came.

The basis of our faith, according to the end of John 16:27, is believing that Christ came from God—believing that Christ is God. Unfortunately, that is one doctrine liberal theologians is willing to give up today. When you give up that, the basis of everything Christians believe in is gone. If Christ isn't God, then we could speculate that everything He said about God's love is a lie. If so, we have nothing to believe in and no divine love at all. We must accept the fact that Jesus Christ is God incarnate. It is the cardinal doctrine of everything we know, believe in, and hope for. Christ is not merely a man. If He were, the claims He made about His deity and God's love were lies. But Jesus *is* God.

Second Peter 2:1-2 says that those who deny the Lord are heretics. In Galatians 1 Paul expresses concern over those who preached falsehoods about Christ. First John 4:3 says that every spirit that does not acknowledge Jesus Christ is from God is the spirit of the antichrist. According to 2 John 10, anyone who presents a different Christ is not to be given welcome. We must commit ourselves to the basic doctrine of the gospel: that Jesus Christ is none other than God in human flesh.

2. Believing in Christ's redemptive work

John 16:27 tells of God's special love for those who "have believed that [Christ] came out from God." Why did God send Christ? To redeem man. Our faith requires us to believe not only in the deity of Christ but also that Christ was sent from God to accomplish the redemption of man. So we who are Christians don't just believe in love, music, religion, or church. We believe in God's revelation of Himself in Christ to do a redemptive work in the world. And the real commitment of faith comes not when you just believe the truth about Christ but when you love Him. James 2:19 says that the demons believe in God and tremble. Belief is not commitment unless it is backed up with a love for the Lord. I believe the truth about Christ. I love Him, and that secures my faith.

Jesus says in John 8:24, "If ye believe not that I am he, ye shall die in your sins." What did He mean when He said, "If ye believe not that I am *he?*" (emphasis added). He was referring to all that He claimed to be: the way, the truth, the life (John 14:6), the bread of life (John 6:35), the light of the world (John 8:12), the resurrection and the life (John 11:25), and God in human flesh (John 10:30, 33). Unless you believe Christ is God, you are mocking Him. And not only are we to believe, but we are to back up our belief with love.

Falling Passionately in Love with Christ

Pastor Daniel Poling told this story about a relative of his, the American novelist and dramatist Channing Pollock. Mr. Pollock and another author were working on a play late one night in Mr. Pollock's New York apartment. Somehow their conversation led the author to ask Mr. Pollock, "Have you ever read the New Testament?" Pollock admitted that he had never read it, and after that brief exchange, nothing more was said about it. After the friend left in the early hours of the morning, Pollock went to bed. He couldn't sleep, however, because he kept thinking about the comment his friend made about reading the New Testament. Finally he got out of bed and searched his books for a New

Testament. He found one and read straight through the gospel of Mark. Afterwards he walked the streets of Manhattan until dawn. He later told Daniel Poling that when he returned to his apartment exhausted, he found himself on his knees passionately in love with Jesus Christ. That's the commitment of true faith. Salvation is initiated by belief in Christ, but true saving faith is expressed by a love that backs up our belief.

C. A Call for Faith

1. The announcement from Christ

a) A clear presentation of the truth about Himself

In John 16:28 Jesus says, "I came forth from the Father, and am come into the world; again, I leave the world, and go to the Father." Christ's existence is a fact of history. That He came from the Father speaks of His deity. He existed in heaven and came into a sin-cursed world. The absolute, historical revelation of God in Christ is basic to saving faith. Jesus came from God, and He was God in human flesh. We can't do away with that doctrine, or the basis of our faith becomes nothing.

(1) The truth rejected

The Jewish religious leaders of the New Testament era didn't love Christ. They didn't even believe He came from God. That is evidenced in John 8:14, where Christ tells them, "Though I bear witness of myself, yet my witness is true; for I know from where I came, and where I go; but ye cannot tell from where I come, and where I go." The Jewish religious leaders were the scholars on religious matters in that part of the world, but they didn't know anything about Christ. They didn't know where He came from or where He was going.

(2) The truth proved

> In John chapter 1 we read, "In the beginning was the Word [Christ], and the Word was with God, and the Word was God. . . . He was in the world, and the world was made by him, and the world knew him not. He came unto his own, and his own received him not" (vv. 1, 10-11). The people Christ came to didn't know who He was, where He came from, why He came, or where He was going. They didn't understand the redemptive plan of God. Jesus says in John 16:28 that He "came forth from the Father." He is nothing less than God in human flesh. He wasn't just a human being, a revolutionary, or a religious freak. He is God come into the world.

b) A clear presentation of the truth of the gospel

John 16:28 is the most concise statement Jesus ever uttered in regard to His origin and destiny. He had told the disciples before in vague terms that He came from God and would go back to Him. But John 16:28 clearly proclaims that Christ came from God to do His perfect, redemptive work for mankind, then went back to God. The entire gospel message is contained in John 16:28.

Some of the earlier statements Christ made about His relationship with God weren't clear. In John 16:5 He says, "Now I go my way to him that sent me." Then in verse 16 He says, "A little while, and ye shall not see me; and again, a little while, and ye shall see me, because I go to the Father." Those statements didn't make much sense to the disciples. In John 14:28 the Lord says, "Ye have heard how I said unto you, I go away, and come again unto you. If ye loved me, ye would rejoice, because I said, I go unto the Father; for my Father is greater than I." That was a confusing statement, too. But in John 16:28, Christ makes a straightforward statement that speaks of Christ's purpose on earth and His identity as God.

It's beautiful to realize from verse 28 that Jesus wasn't a puppet who came and went at the whims of an outside force. There weren't any hostile powers that forced Jesus to leave earth. He wasn't running in fear from persecution, nor was the Father calling Him home. He came to teach man about God and to die on the cross. When His work on earth was finished, He returned to God. By His own will He completed His mission and returned to the place He came from. John 16:28 speaks of God's existence. It speaks of a God who loves man and became human to accomplish a redemptive work, then returned so they could be energized by the Spirit to live the life He provided for them.

2. The apprehension by the disciples

In John 16:29 we read, "His disciples said unto him, Lo, now speakest thou plainly, and speakest no proverb." They were saying, "Now we understand, Lord! We're finally beginning to comprehend what You're talking about." Perhaps the disciples thought Christ's earlier prophetic statement about the day when He would no longer speak in proverbs (v. 25) was fulfilled at that moment. They understood Christ's words about His work, origin, and destiny (v. 28), but they wouldn't actually have full understanding of all Christ's veiled statements until the Spirit's coming on the Day of Pentecost (Acts 2:4).

The disciples grasp the meaning of Jesus' simple statement in verse 28 and probably feel good about that. We can see the simplicity of their faith by their response in verse 29. They could see that God loved them, that He sent Christ to redeem them, and that Christ was going back to God when He finished His work. God's divine plan was becoming clear. Jesus came, loved them, and opened up the way to God. Once they had access to God's presence, Christ went back to God.

Although the disciples had a new understanding regarding Christ, they still didn't understand Christ's words in verse 28 as much as they would later on. John Calvin said of the disciples' response in John 16:29, "It is certain that the disciples did not yet understand fully the meaning of Christ's discourse; but though they were not yet capable of this, the mere odour of it refreshed them" (*Commentary on the Gospel of John*, vol. 2 [Grand Rapids: Baker, reprint 1979], p. 161). The disciples were beginning to understand Christ. Of course, they still didn't have full understanding until the Holy Spirit came; but they were making progress, because for the first time that we can tell, the disciples stopped being sorrowful. They took their attention off their problems long enough to be excited about what they were learning, and they believed all that they understood.

How Can I Believe What I Don't Understand?

All God ever asks from a man is that he believe what he understands. Frequently people ask questions such as, How did the people in the book of Genesis become saved? Did the people who lived in the era of 1 and 2 Kings know how to become saved? What about other people in the Old Testament?

Men were saved by believing the revelation of God at whatever point it had been disclosed. God didn't expect those in the book of Genesis to know and believe the revelations that were given in the New Testament era. God expects people to believe only what they are able to understand from the revelations He has given up to that point in time. We don't need to know all the answers; we just need to believe what God has told us. True saving faith is a commitment to everything that God has revealed to you. The Old Testament saints didn't know exactly how God's redemptive work would be done. But they believed God's promise to redeem them. They believed only what they understood. And Jesus didn't expect the disciples to understand everything He said in John 16. But His statements weren't said in vain; the disciples would have full understanding later on.

D. A Confession of Faith

In John 16:30 the disciples say, "Now are we sure that thou knowest all things, and needest not that any man should ask thee; by this we believe that thou camest forth from God." They were asserting their confidence in Christ's deity.

1. The ironic event

A few hours after the disciples asserted Christ's deity, the disciples ran away like a flock of fearful sheep when Jesus was arrested. They said they were sure that Christ was all He claimed to be, but later on they weren't so sure. As Christians, we've all experienced those moments of doubt. We begin to mistrust God and say, "Does God really exist? Is what the Bible says for real?" Then we get over the doubt and regain our confidence that God is all He claims to be. The disciples were no different. Their faith may have been more infantile, thus making them more susceptible to doubt. But in John 16:30, they are sure that Christ knew all things.

2. The indisputable evidence

The disciples had recently realized how much Christ knew because earlier (in John 16:17-19) He answered a question they hadn't even asked. The disciples had already seen evidence that Christ was who He claimed to be, but what finally convinced them was the fact that He knew everything. Consequently, they said, "We believe that thou camest forth from God." They made a statement of their belief in Christ's deity. And we know that the disciples also loved Christ. Their belief and love was sufficient for saving faith.

Some people wonder if the profession the disciples made in John 16:30 determines their actual conversion. I don't know if we can really pinpoint when they became saved. I think they believed in Christ prior to John 16, and that in John 16 they simply gained a better understanding of who He was. They had believed in His divine origin and His deity, and they had shown Him again and again how much they loved Him. That's the essence of salvation: believing and loving Christ. In saying, "We believe that thou camest forth from God," the disciples confessed that they saw the glory of His deity shining through the veil of His humanity. Their understanding was as clear as it had ever been in the three years they had spent with Christ.

How Much Faith Do I Need to Become Saved?

After the resurrection, the disciples' faith became even greater. John 16:30 marks the apex of their faith prior to Christ's death. The disciples struggled with doubt during Christ's trial and death, but their faith was still present within them. And when Jesus came out of the grave, their faith shone more brightly than it ever had shone. The child-like faith they express in John 16 is like the faith of the man in Mark 9:24 who says, "Lord, I believe; help thou mine unbelief." With their doubts, fears, and misgivings, Jesus accepted them as they were. That's how He accepts you, too. Some people say, "I want to become a Christian, but I have some questions. I have some fears; I don't understand everything." Christ is willing to accept you at the point you express your infant faith.

It's important to keep in mind that the disciples' faith had content. They believed that Jesus came from God to accomplish work here on earth and that He would go back to God afterward. Believing is a matter of putting your faith in something and someone, not in nothing. Faith must have content.

E. The Celebration over Faith

In John 16:31 the Lord says to the disciples, "Do ye now believe?" That is not really a question; it was a response to the disciples' confession in verse 30. He was saying, "Now you believe. That's great; I accept your faith." Christ must have been happy when the disciples professed their belief in Him (v. 30), because He had been teaching them about Himself for three years. The reality of the disciples' salvation appears to come to a climax. We can't dogmatically say Christ was speaking factually and not asking a question. But the context of Christ's words seems to call for a factual statement.

In John 16:31, Christ is experiencing a moment of sweet victory because from the time the disciples begin to express their sorrow in John 14, He struggled to make them trust Him in the midst of the bitter news of His departure. Finally, the sunlight of faith began to break in the disciples' hearts, and smiles replaced their sorrow. Their infantile faith was enough for Jesus. After three years of miracles, teaching, and loving, and a full evening of giving Himself to comfort the disciples, they finally said, "We believe." For Jesus, that was enough. They didn't have full-grown faith; nevertheless, they believed. As we said earlier, Jesus doesn't ask that we come to Him with total comprehension. He asks only that we come with infantile faith and say, "I believe; help me in my unbelief" (cf. Mark 9:24).

F. A Caution About Faith

When the disciples told Jesus, "We believe that thou camest forth from God," they were confident in the strength of their faith. That is made evident in verse 32, which is a warning. So in verse 31-32 Christ basically says, "Now you believe. But there is going to come a time when your faith is tested." The disciples thought they were immovable rocks when they were really like pebbles. In John 13:37 Peter says he is willing to die for Jesus. But in John 18, Peter denies Christ three times. He failed to realize the infancy of his faith and the weakness of his flesh. Likewise, in John 16 the disciples as a whole fail to recognize Satan's power and the weakness of their faith. They were like young military recruits who knew the drill instructions but not what to do when they got into battle. We have to remember that the secrecy of spiritual strength is self-distrust and deep humility. Paul says in 2 Corinthians 12:10, "When I am weak, then am I strong." When you recognize your weakness, you will be strong.

1. The fickleness of man

Jesus begins John 16:32 by saying, "Behold, the hour cometh, yea, is now come, that ye shall be scattered, every man to his own, and shall leave me alone." In Matthew 26:56, we read that the disciples fled when Jesus was arrested. That fulfilled the prophecy in Zechariah 13:7: "Smite the shepherd, and the sheep shall be scattered." It is sad that Jesus had to state that warning. Does the fleeing of the disciples prove that their faith was a sham? No. Their faith was shaken badly, but they still had some faith. When Christ rose from the dead, their faith was stirred again and bore fruit.

I like the way the disciples are honestly portrayed in John 16:32. The Bible frequently reminds us that the greatest saints were people like you and me. They weren't super-spiritual, pious heroes. They lacked faith at times. The disciples were barely hanging onto a thread of faith when Christ was crucified. But after the resurrection, Christ fanned their faith again, and they set the world on fire for Him.

2. The faithfulness of the Father

John 16:32 concludes with this statement from Jesus: "Yet I am not alone, because the Father is with me." The disciples would soon leave Christ, but the Father would be with Him. For the first time in the Upper Room discourse with the disciples, Christ reflected on His own anguish. He sadly told the disciples that they would all leave Him. Thinking of His loneliness, He said, "The Father will be with Me." Did you know that even the Father left Christ for a brief period of time? When Christ was on the cross bearing all the sins of the world, He said, "Eli, Eli, lama sabachthani? that is to say, My God, my God, why hast thou forsaken me?" (Matt. 27:46). Our holy Father couldn't look upon Christ when He bore the sins of the world.

The dialogue in John 16:28-32 gives us wonderful insights into the Lord Jesus and the level of the disciples' faith. We learn there is something to believe in, even if with infantile faith: that Jesus is God in human flesh, and that He came to earth to do a redemptive work. He died on the cross for us and then returned to the Father. That's all we need to believe, despite any doubts and misgivings we might have. When you believe Christ, He will receive your faith as it is and strengthen it. There will be times when sin and temptation may cause your faith to wane, but Christ will fan the flame of your faith and strengthen it again.

Faith is believing in Jesus and all that He claimed to be. We can believe in God's love because He revealed it to us in Jesus Christ. You can bet your life on His love.

III. HOPE (v. 33)

A. The Proclamation of Hope

Jesus says to the disciples in John 16:33, "These things I have spoken unto you, that in me ye might have peace. In the world ye shall have tribulation: but be of good cheer; I have overcome the world." What fantastic hope that gives us! In John 15 the Lord warns the disciples that the world would persecute them. In John 16:2 He says, "The time cometh, that whosoever killeth you will think that he doeth God service." The world is hopeless; war, pollution, and disaster surround us. Is there any escape from the plagues of man? Yes. Jesus said, "Be of good cheer; I have overcome the world."

When you know and love Jesus Christ, there is hope. This world holds no fears for us. People talk about the terrible disasters that will come about in the future. I don't believe Christians will ever experience them, because Christ takes care of His own. I'm confident that before any catastrophic disasters happen, Jesus will take us out of this world in the rapture. We have the hope of living in eternity with Christ someday.

B. The Passages on Hope

Satan gave Christ his best shots when Jesus was on the cross, and the Lord took every one. He went into the grave and emerged the victor from the other side of the grave. He defeated Satan and conquered the power of death (1 Cor. 15:54). Jesus said, "Because I live, ye shall live also" (John 14:19). We can put our hope in that. Just as a mountain guide reaches a flat area and pulls up to safety an ascending climber, so Jesus is a conqueror who is pulling us to Him. He won the victory and shares it with us. Paul says in 1 Corinthians 15:55, "O death, where is thy sting? O grave, where is thy victory?"

According to Romans 8:37, we are "more than conquerors through him that loved us." Nothing can separate us from the Lord's love (v. 35). That is our hope. Someday we will leave this world to be with Jesus Christ. And we don't need to fear the world because Christ has overcome it. First John 5:5 says, "Who is he that overcometh the world, but he that believeth that Jesus is the Son of God?" If you believe in Christ, you are an overcomer—just as He is!

Conclusion

When you know faith, hope, and love, you will have peace. Jesus said, "These things [faith, hope, and love] I have spoken unto you, that in me ye might have peace" (v. 33). In John 15:11 Jesus tells the disciples, "These things have I spoken unto you, that my joy might remain in you." The result of peace is joy.

Is it possible to know peace in a world like ours? Yes, because God loves you. And you'll know peace when you love Him. We can believe in God and the gift of eternal salvation. The hope God offers is steadfast and secure. He gives the hope of eternal life in His presence. Because of that, we can have perfect peace and joy through Jesus Christ.

Focusing on the Facts

1. Give some examples of how people live by faith (see p. 85).
2. What certainty can man put his faith in? Explain (John 16:27; see pp. 85-86).
3. What is the basis of the Christian faith? What does Scripture say about those who don't acknowledge that truth (see pp. 86-87)?
4. Why did Christ come forth from God (see p. 87)?
5. Belief is not commitment unless it is backed up with _____ (see p. 87).
6. What did Jesus mean when He said, "If ye believe not that I am *he*?" (John 8:24, emphasis added; see p. 87).

7. What verification do we see of Christ's deity in John 1:1, 10-11 (see p. 89)?
8. Discuss the clarity and significance of what Jesus says in John 16:28 (see pp. 89-90).
9. Does God ask a person to believe what he doesn't understand? Explain (see p. 91).
10. In John 16:30, the disciples profess Christ's deity. What helped convince them to the point of making that profession (see p. 92)?
11. What kind of faith is Christ willing to accept from us? What must we keep in mind about whether a person's faith is acceptable (see p. 93)?
12. In John 16:32, Jesus warns the disciples that their faith is not as strong as they think it is. Does the fact that they fled when Jesus was arrested prove that they had no faith? Explain (see p. 95).
13. Discuss the hope we have of victory over death and the world (see p. 97).
14. What will you have when you know faith, hope, and love? What then follows (John 16:33; see p. 97)?

Pondering the Principles

1. For a better understanding of faith, let's look at what Hebrews 11:1 says: "Faith is the assurance of things hoped for, the conviction of things not seen" (NASB). Faith is trusting in a hope or a promise that is so real, it gives assurance. With that in mind, read Hebrews 11:3-13, which lists a number of Old Testament saints who rested on the promises of God. How did those people express their faith?

2. Satan frequently tries to make Christians doubt God and His promises. One way we can defend ourselves against such doubt is to learn all that we can about God's character and His promises. When you don't know what God is like or what His promises are, then Satan will try to create doubt out of your ignorance. During the next two weeks, make a project of writing down everything you learn about God's character and His promises whenever you read your Bible. You might also be able to use the sermons at your church or good Christian books as resources of information. You'll find the knowledge of God's character and His promises to be a great faith-builder!

6

Let Me Alone; I Can't Cope

Outline

Introduction
A. The Inability to Cope with Life
B. The Illustration for Coping with Life
   1. Paul's qualification to be an illustration
   2. Our qualification to be an illustration

Lesson
I. The Principles (vv. 1-7)
  A. Have an Adequate Stand (v. 1b)
    1. The coexistence
      a) The explanation
      b) The extent
    2. The challenge
      a) The failure to stand strong
        (1) The Israelites' example
        (2) King David's example
          (a) His dependence on human wisdom
          (b) His departure from human wisdom
      b) The formula for standing strong
  B. Have an Adequate Love (vv. 1-3)
    1. The expression of love (v. 1a, c)
    2. The encouragement of love (v. 2)
      a) The problem
      b) The plea
    3. The exhortation to love
      a) The request (v. 3a)
      b) The reason (v. 3b)

C. Have an Adequate Joy (v. 4)
  1. The method
  2. The manner
D. Have an Adequate Gentleness (v. 5a)
  1. The expression of gentleness
  2. The example of gentleness
E. Have an Adequate Security (vv. 5b-7)
  1. Explaining security
  2. Exemplifying security
II. The Practice (vv. 8-9)

Conclusion

Introduction

A. The Inability to Cope with Life

In a book entitled *Mastery*, Methodist missionary E. Stanley Jones wrote, "The art of living is the least learned of all arts. Man has learned the art of existing, of getting by somehow with the demands of life, of escaping into half answers; but he knows little about the art of living . . . with all its demands" ([Nashville: Abingdon], p. v).

Many people cannot cope with life. Even Christians sometimes have a hard time living a fulfilled, happy life—a life where from morning to night everything is great. How can we have that kind of life? A look at Philippians 4 will tell us the answer.

B. The Illustration for Coping with Life

In this lesson, we're going to study Paul's example of how to cope with life. He was a person such as we are, and his example will help us. He wasn't divine; he was human. Christ gives us a perfect example of victory in coping with life, but we need to study the life of a sinner who attained victory after failing. Christ is our Savior, and Paul is our

---

Note: The outline and some of the thoughts in this lesson were suggested in Paul S. Rees's book *The Adequate Man: Paul in Philippians* (Westwood, N.J.: Revell, 1959).

encourager. He failed in life at times but kept getting back up and moving on.

1. Paul's qualification to be an illustration

Philippians 4:12-13 capsulizes why Paul is a good example for us to learn from. There Paul wrote, "I know both how to be abased, and I know how to abound; everywhere and in all things I am instructed both to be full and to be hungry, both to abound and to suffer need. I can do all things through Christ, who strengtheneth me." If you're looking for someone who experienced much in life, look at Paul. He knew what it was like to have great happiness and to have the worst of problems. He knew how to win and how to lose; he knew what it was like to be well and deathly sick. He had experienced both freedom and chains. Paul had been through almost every circumstance life could give, and he learned how to handle each one. He had been through the worst, the best, and everything in the middle.

In Philippians 4:9 Paul says, "Those things which ye have both learned, and received, and heard, and seen in me, do." He was basically saying, "I've been through the gamut of human experience. Look at how I handled my circumstances and what I've taught you, and follow my example."

2. Our qualification to be an illustration

Paul must have had a lot of confidence to ask people to follow him. Yet every one of us should be able to say that to others. Mothers should be able to say to their daughters, "See the way I live? That's the way you ought to live." Fathers should be able to say that to their sons. Paul ended Philippians 4:9 by telling the Philippians that if they followed his example, the God of peace would be with them.

As a pastor, I should be able to say, "Do the things you've learned from me and seen in my life. If you do, God will bless you." All Christians should be able to say others can follow their example. If you can't say that, it's not because you're unable to live up to God's standard. Every believer has the potential to be what God wants him to be.

So, Paul tells us in Philippians 4 that if we want to learn how to handle varying circumstances in life, we can look to his example. We can watch how he lived and live the same way. In this lesson, we'll look at the principles Paul gave us.

Living as Paul Teaches Us to Live

Why should we live as Paul suggests? Some people will answer it's because that's the way to get blessed. Others say it's because we will be good witnesses, because we will have security about our salvation, or because we will receive a reward when the Lord comes. Those are good answers, but the ultimate reason you should live the godly example portrayed in Philippians 4 is that by doing so, you will glorify God. In Titus 2:10 Paul says we are to "adorn the doctrine of God." God is on trial in the world, and we should live in a way that manifests the truth about Him. When Christians live fulfilled, positive, meaningful lives, that says something about the God who is running their lives. We ought to live by Paul's example for God's sake.

Lesson

I. THE PRINCIPLES (vv. 1-7)

A. Have an Adequate Stand (v. 1b)

"Therefore, my brethren . . . stand fast in the Lord."

The word *therefore* refers to whatever it was Paul previously talked about. Prior to Philippians 4:1, Paul talks about the Lord Jesus Christ and the salvation we have in Him. He talked about the humiliation, exaltation, power, excellency, and resurrection of Christ. He said that Christ is going to change us to become like Him. And because of who Christ is, we are to stand fast in Him. We don't need to be disturbed about our circumstances because we can stand fast in the Lord.

1. The coexistence

   a) The explanation

   Every Christian is in Christ; your life is hid with Christ in God (Col. 3:3). We are all bound up with God, and we share a common eternal life. In Paul's letters, there are 132 references to the fact that the believer is in Christ. In Philippians 3:8-9 he says, "I count all things but loss for the excellency of the knowledge of Christ Jesus, my Lord; for whom I have suffered the loss of all things, and do count them but refuse, that I may win Christ, and be found *in him*, not having mine own righteousness, which is of the law [legalism], but that which is through the faith of Christ, the righteousness which is of God by faith" (emphasis added).

   Being in Christ is coming into union with Him by faith. In 2 Corinthians 5:17 Paul says, "If any man be in Christ, he is a new creation." Life really begins once you're in Christ. There is no life outside of Christ; there is no meaning to life without Him. Christ alone can introduce man to the God of the universe, for whom man was created. So life begins by being in Christ. And how does a person become a part of Christ? By faith (Phil. 3:9). When you accept that Christ died for you and you invite Him to become your Savior, you become one with Him. Whoever is joined to the Lord is one spirit with Him (1 Cor. 6:17).

   b) The extent

   Christ lives in those who are believers, and we live in Him. We are wrapped up with the Person of Jesus Christ. The life you live is not your own; it's the life of Christ within you (Gal. 2:20). The righteousness you have before God is not your own; it is the Lord's, and it was granted to you (Rom. 3:21-26). The love you show to others is God's love, which is shed abroad in your heart (Rom. 5:5). The strength you have to do God's will is given to you through Christ (Phil. 4:13), who is able to "do exceedingly abundantly above all that we ask or think, according to the power that worketh in us" (Eph. 3:20). Everything in our existence is Christ in us. Therein lies our security, life, and righteousness.

Paul is saying in Philippians 4:1, "Every Christian is in Christ. You may have problems in life, but stand fast knowing that you're one with Christ. Whatever is happening to you is happening to Him, and He has the resources to handle your circumstance. Some people might say, What about when we sin? In 1 Corinthians 6:15-16 Paul says that when a Christian joins himself to a prostitute, he joins Christ to the prostitute, too. That's how complete the believer's identification is with Christ. The Lord Himself doesn't sin, but when you sin you drag His presence into your sin because you are one with Him. If Christ is with us when we sin, that means He's also with us when we are in difficult circumstances. You can take comfort knowing that He's with you. Stand fast in the Lord. Without God, you don't have anything to lean on for support.

2. The challenge

Are you standing fast in the Lord both positionally and practically? You are standing fast positionally if you've come to Jesus Christ; you are secure in Him. But there are many Christians who aren't standing fast practically. They waver when they encounter problems. It's important that we put into practice what is true about us positionally. In Galatians 5:1 Paul says, "Stand fast, therefore, in the liberty with which Christ hath made us free." He was telling the Galatians, "Don't go back to your legalistic life-style of trying to be religious by following rules. Instead, stand firm in your new freedom by being obedient to the Spirit of God as you're led by Him." That Paul commands us to stand fast indicates there are some Christians who aren't standing fast. First Corinthians

16:13 says, "Stand firm in the faith, act like men, be strong" (NASB). There is nothing in the universe that can remove from us our secure positional stand in the Lord, but there are plenty of Christians who allow themselves to get knocked in their Christian walk by their circumstances.

In 2 Thessalonians 2:15 Paul writes, "Therefore, brethren, stand fast, and hold the traditions which ye have been taught, whether by word or our epistle." Our stand is based on the Word of God. In Ephesians 6, where we read about the armor of the believer, verse 15 says you are to have your feet "shod with the preparation of the gospel of peace." A soldier who is in battle needs the right kind of shoes so he can stand firm. The point of the armor is that having done all, we are to stand (Eph. 6:13). In regard to the shoes in verse 15, the emphasis is not on going out to preach the gospel, but on standing fast. Those shoes are what give you solid footing.

What will help us to stand firm? The "gospel of peace" (Eph. 6:15). That's a reference to the fact that believers are at peace with God (Rom. 5:1). Satan will try to shoot us down and make us doubt the security of our salvation, question if God really cares about us, or wonder if we can be victorious in life. But if you have your feet shod right, you'll be able to tell Satan, "Hold it! I am at peace with God; He is on my side." We who are believers are at peace with God; He's on our team. We used to be rebels, but not anymore. What do we have to worry about? God is on our side. If Satan attacks, we've got God to help us.

a) The failure to stand strong

(1) The Israelites' example

In Numbers 13-14, the Israelites felt inadequate about facing the enemies before them in the Promised Land. They said the people in the land were giants, and they saw themselves as grasshoppers (Num. 13:33). As a result of their refusal to stand strong, they died in the wilderness. They didn't trust that God could handle the giant people in the Promised Land. They didn't stand fast in the Lord; instead, they stood fast in human wisdom, and that wouldn't hold them up. Humanly, they didn't have the military resources to handle their enemies. But that was the wrong resource to depend on. When you have a problem in your life, you have to get away from human confusion and stand on God's character.

(2) King David's example

In 1 Samuel 21 is an interesting account of how King David handled a specific circumstance in his life. Keep in mind that he had slain more than ten thousand men in battle (1 Sam. 18:7). He had written psalm after psalm and, more than anyone else in the Old Testament, had spelled out the character of God. He was a brilliant musician and poet. He was a great man of God, and he knew victory after victory in battle.

(a) His dependence on human wisdom

However, in 1 Samuel 21:10 we read that one day "David arose, and fled . . . for fear of Saul." David was afraid of Saul. He didn't remember that God was on his side and that God was stronger than Saul. All he thought about was that Saul was after him. We could apply to him what Martin Luther told Erasmus: "Your thoughts concerning God are too human" (*The Bondage of the Will* [Grand Rapids: Baker, issued 1976], p. 50). When you think wrongly of God, you come up with a God who doesn't exist, and you end up with atheism. Christians who don't stand strong are atheists in practice, because by their actions they are denying that God can handle their problems.

David in his fear ran to Philistia, which wasn't the friendliest place to go. He went to King Achish of Gath. Verses 11-13 tell us what happened: "The servants of Achish said unto [Achish], Is not this David the king of the land? Did they not sing one to another of him in dances, saying, Saul hath slain his thousands, and David his ten thousands? And David laid up these words in his heart, and was very much afraid of Achish, the king of Gath. And he changed his behavior before them, and feigned himself mad in their hands, and made marks on the doors of the gate, and let his spittle fall down upon his beard." David pretended to be crazy. He started slobbering and scratching at things. How undignified for a king of Israel! David had forgotten that God was on his side.

When David got panicky and started acting crazy, Achish said, "Have I need of mad men, that ye have brought this fellow to play the mad man in my presence?" (1 Sam. 21:15).

(b) His departure from human wisdom

David was able to get away from Achish, and he escaped to the cave of Adullam (22:1). There he wrote Psalm 57. He said, "Be merciful unto me, O God, be merciful unto me; for my soul trusteth in thee. Yea, in the shadow of thy wings will I make my refuge" (v. 1). David couldn't go to Philistia because of Achish, and he couldn't return to Israel because of Saul. He had only one place to go—to God. While he was in the cave, he came to his senses again. He says in Psalm 57:7, "My heart is fixed, O God, my heart is fixed." His heart became fixed on God. He knew he didn't have the answer to his dilemma and finally looked to God for the answer. The psalm continues, "I will sing and give praise. Awake up, my glory; awake, psaltery and harp" (vv. 7-8). David was telling himself to smile and be happy. Did his circumstance change? No, but he began to reaffirm to his own heart that he had a God who could solve his problem.

b) The formula for standing strong

When you don't understand your circumstances but you know who God is, you can remain standing. Ephesians 6:10 tells us to "be strong in the Lord, and in the power of his might." What an incredible resource the Christian has! When troubles come your way, you can stand strong on God's character. Sometimes people will come to me and say, "I have such-and-such a problem. What book should I read to help me?" They'll expect an answer such as, "Here's a book on depression," or, "Here's a book on self-evaluation." But usually I'll recommend a book that will give them a better understanding of God. We need to know who our resource is. It's good to know God in His fullness. Paul continually pursued a greater knowledge of the Lord (Phil. 3:10). Study the truth of God and His character, for on that you can stand in the midst of any trial. Paul stood fast in the Lord in all kinds of bad circumstances because he had confidence in Him. He even sang in the Philippian jail (Acts 16:25).

B. Have an Adequate Love (vv. 1-3)

1. The expression of love (v. 1*a, c*)

"My brethren dearly beloved and longed for, my joy and crown . . . my dearly beloved."

Paul was full of love for the Philippians. But who exactly are the people he's writing to? Two of them are mentioned in the next verse.

2. The encouragement of love (v. 2)

"I beseech Euodia, and beseech Syntyche, that they be of the same mind in the Lord."

a) The problem

The name *Euodia* means "sweet fragrance," and *Syntyche* means "pleasant." Apparently those women weren't living up to their names. Instead they were troublesome and were threatening the unity in the Philippian church.

b) The plea

A church split is a tragic thing. Not only is it a bad testimony, but it also leaves scars for everyone involved. It breaks God's heart when His people can't get along. There are times when a church needs to split. If apostasy introduces itself, the truth needs to walk away. But when good, honest Christians fight each other and the church is fractured, then there's a lot of heartache. Paul especially would have experienced pain over this circumstance, because he had poured his heart into the Philippian church. He had paid a high price to get those people to know Jesus Christ, and he didn't want two women destroying the church by causing problems.

Paul could have told the Philippians to take those women and send them somewhere else. Instead, he said, "I beseech." He didn't command that the women be rebuked; he simply asked that a plea be made for unity.

3. The exhortation to love

a) The request (v. 3*a*)

"I entreat thee also, true yokefellow, help those women."

It's possible that when Paul said "yokefellow," he had in mind a specific person in the Philippian congregation, but we can't be too certain. The Greek word for "yokefellow," *suzugos,* does appear elsewhere in Greek literature as a proper name. It could be that he was asking someone in the congregation to help Euodia and Syntyche.

b) The reason (v. 3*b*)

"Help those women who labored with me in the gospel, with Clement also, and with other my fellow workers, whose names are in the book of life."

The two women Paul had labored with Paul in the gospel. They apparently had a prominent role in the church. And he wanted them to get back into unity again.

You shouldn't love only the people that help you build up the church; you should also love the people who want to break up the church. Don't just love those who want to pat you on the back but love those who want to stab you in the back as well. True love is indiscriminate. The love of God shed abroad in our hearts (Rom. 5:5) is to be given to all men. Paul loved Euodia and Syntyche in addition to Barnabas, Silas, and others. If God loved only the lovely, who would receive His love? Paul loved the two quarrelsome women in the Philippian church.

You'll never know the meaning of life until you learn how to love with a Christlike love. Real living involves real loving. Only those who love others enjoy and know life. Many people today are sour, warped, and unhappy because they can't forget the things they hate. It's better to love everyone. You may say, "But if I love that way, I'll get burned." Yes, but you'll be able to love in spite of what happens. Paul said to the Colossians, "Put off all these: anger, wrath, malice, blasphemy, [and slander] . . . . Put on, therefore, as the elect of God, holy and beloved, tender mercies, kindness, humbleness of mind, meekness, long-suffering, forbearing one another. . . . And above all these things put on love, which is the bond of perfectness" (Col. 3:8, 12-14). We are to have an adequate love, and that love comes from God.

C. Have an Adequate Joy (v. 4)

"Rejoice in the Lord always; and again I say, Rejoice."

Paul's statement is a command. Have you ever seen Philippians 4:4 in that light? We can go up to a believer who's perpetually miserable and say, "Did you know that the New Testament repeatedly commands us to rejoice?" One of the principles for living a fulfilled life is to rejoice.

1. The method

Do you want to be happy and know fulfillment? Rejoice. Someone might say, "But you don't know my circumstances." Paul wasn't talking about circumstances in Philippians 4:4. He didn't say, "Rejoice in your circumstances always." He said to rejoice in the Lord. Does the Lord ever cause you to lose joy? He shouldn't, because He never changes from all that He is now. People become unhappy in life because their happiness is dependent upon their circumstances rather than upon the Lord.

Paul had a supernatural resource. He was plugged into the Lord—and He knew that the Lord doesn't change (Mal. 3:6). Paul was always happy because He could trust the Lord's consistency in the midst of circumstances that came and went. His joy was in the Lord, and his circumstances couldn't touch that joy. Voltaire once exclaimed that men are "tormented atoms in a bit of mud, devoured by death, a mockery of fate. This world, this theatre of pride and wrong, swarms with sick fools who talk of happiness" (quoted by W. P. King in *The Search for Happiness* [Nashville: Abingdon], p. 9). What an unhappy attitude to have in life! There aren't many happy people in the world, because you can't know true happiness apart from the Lord. People tend to base their joy on the exhilaration of their circumstance, but the Christian's joy is predicated on the unchanging nature of his Lord and on what the Lord has done for him.

2. The manner

Our joy should be incessant. Paul said, "Rejoice in the Lord *always*" (emphasis added). We can go into the Lord's presence and be happy with who He is when we are in the middle of painful circumstances. Paul had unceasing tears for the Israelites (Rom. 9:2-3) and the Ephesians (Acts 20:31). He knew sorrow, but on the inside his joy was constant. Would you like to have such joy? It's easy—all you need to do is walk in the Spirit. (Walking in the Spirit is basically living in full submission to God's Word and making constant confession of your sin.) Romans 14:17 says, "The kingdom of God is not food and drink, but righteousness, and peace, and joy in the Holy Spirit." Joy is a by-product of walking in the Spirit. And joy is also connected to love. Jesus said, "If you loved me, ye would rejoice" (John 14:28). Those who love are happy. Have you ever noticed that when people fall in love they bubble over with happiness? In a divine sense, the same thing happens when your heart is filled with love for God: You will have overflowing joy!

D. Have an Adequate Gentleness (v. 5a)

"Let your moderation [gentleness] be known unto all men."

1. The expression of gentleness

I like the Phillips translation, which paraphrases this verse to say, "Have a reputation for gentleness" (London: Bles, 1960). It bothers me that there are some people who think I'm somewhat bombastic because I talk loudly and firmly when I preach. That's because I have strong convictions. Maybe I give the impression that I plow through people with those convictions.

It's good to be strong about your convictions, just as Jesus cleansed the Temple in righteous indignation (John 2:13-16), but you still have to be gentle with people. In 2 Corinthians 10:1, Paul speaks of the gentleness of Christ. Our Lord was gentle with prostitutes and other sinners. The only people He didn't show gentleness to were false teachers. Gentleness is one element of the fruit of the Spirit (Gal. 5:22). Second Timothy 2:24 says, "The servant of the Lord must not strive, but be gentle unto all men." We can't go through the world whacking away at people with our spiritual swords.

2. The example of gentleness

In 1 Thessalonians 2:3-7 Paul speaks to the Thessalonians about how he and his coworkers had first approached them: "Our exhortation was not of deceit, nor of uncleanness, nor in guile; but as we were allowed of God to be put in trust with the gospel, even so we speak; not as pleasing men but God, who testeth our hearts. For neither at any time used we flattering words, as ye know, nor a cloak of covetousness, God is witness; nor of men sought we glory. . . . But we were *gentle* among you, even as a [nursing mother] cherisheth her children" (emphasis added). Paul compared the way he ministered to the way a nursing mother cherishes her baby. The Greek word translated "cherish" means "to warm with body heat." Paul illustrated his gentleness to that of a mother tenderly breast-feeding her infant; that's the kind of gentleness he showed to the pagan Thessalonians.

I know some Christians who are so zealous for the truth, they don't have any gentleness. Instead of attracting people to the gospel, they drive them away. They offend people not by their message but by their lack of gentleness. Gentle people are happy because they don't go around warring against others. Instead, they are peacemakers. It's healthy to be gentle.

E. Have an Adequate Security (vv. 5b-7)

"The Lord is at hand. Be anxious for nothing, but in everything, by prayer and supplication with thanksgiving, let your requests be made known unto God. And the peace of God, which passeth all understanding, shall keep your hearts and minds through Christ Jesus."

1. Explaining security

The phrase "the Lord is at hand" has nothing to do with the second coming. Rather, Paul is saying, "Don't worry; the Lord is here with you. Don't think He's off somewhere else." It's exciting to know we don't have to worry because the Lord is in our presence.

2. Exemplifying security

The following illustrations are from Paul S. Rees's *The Adequate Man: Paul in Philippians* (pp. 104-6):

During Stalin's administration, a group of Russian peasants met in secret for worship. Some soldiers barged in on the meeting and wrote down the name of every person present. When they were done, an elderly man said, "There is one name you have not got." A soldier replied that he had all the names. The peasant insisted that he didn't, and when asked who it was, the peasant replied, "The Lord Jesus Christ!" He knew of the Lord's presence.

During World War II, a missionary whose ship had been torpedoed was picked up by a German ship. He was put into the hold. When asked how he got through the night, he replied, "I began communing with the Lord. He reminded me of his Word in the 121st Psalm: 'My help cometh from the Lord, which made heaven and earth. He will not suffer thy foot to be moved: he that keepeth thee will not slumber. Behold he . . . shall neither slumber or sleep' (vv. 2-4). . . . So I said, 'Lord, there isn't really any use for both of us to stay awake tonight. If You are going to keep watch, I'll thank Thee for some sleep!'"

The Lord is at hand. No matter what happens in your life, He's there with you. He has the resources and power you need. If you perceive God incorrectly, you'll short-circuit your joy. I try to look at troubling circumstances as great opportunities for God to display Himself.

How can we get to the place where we have an adequate stand in the Lord? How can we love everyone with an adequate love and sense an adequate joy that rejoices in God's unchanging character? How do we become adequately gentle and confident of the Lord's presence?

II. THE PRACTICE (vv. 8-9)

"Brethren, whatever things are true, whatever things are honest, whatever things are just, whatever things are pure, whatever things are lovely, whatever things are of good report; if there be any virtue, and if there be any praise, think on these things. Those things which ye have both learned, and received, and heard, and seen in me, do, and the God of peace shall be with you."

Paul is saying that you must set your mind on divine truth, which is true, honest, just, pure, lovely, and of good report. When you do that, you will find that you'll get to know God. That's the key to having a fulfilling life.

Where do you set your mind? Where do you spend the hours of your day? Do you feed on the Word and study it? Do you pass on what you learn to others, thus making it more indelible in your own mind? As you think on the things that reveal God, you'll be able to stand on His character, love with His love, rejoice because of who He is, manifest His kind of gentleness, and stand secure in His presence. If you aren't doing all those things, then your God is too small. The only way you'll enlarge Him is by understanding the revelation that He has given of Himself in His Word.

Conclusion

Think over these words quoted by Paul Rees (p. 111):

> I cannot know why suddenly the storm
> Should rage so fiercely round me in its wrath;
> But this I know—God watches all my path,
>   And I can trust.
>
> I may not draw aside the mystic veil
> That hides the unknown future from my sight,
> Nor know if for me waits the dark or light;
>   But I can trust.

I have no power to look across the tide,
To see while here the land beyond the river;
But this I know—I shall be God's forever;
I can trust!

That's the essence of the fulfilled life: to know God so well that you trust Him in everything and you know and are characterized by undiminished security, gentleness, love, joy, and confidence.

Focusing on the Facts

1. Why is Paul a good example for us in learning how to handle the different circumstances in life (Phil. 4:12-13; see p. 103)?
2. What are some reasons to live as Paul suggests (see p. 104)?
3. Discuss the significance of Paul's statement "If any man be in Christ, he is a new creation" (2 Cor. 5:17; see p. 105).
4. Using Scripture, describe the extent of the Christian's relationship to Christ (see pp. 105-6).
5. Is every Christian standing fast positionally in the Lord? How about practically? Explain (see pp. 106-7).
6. We are to stand firm by having our feet "shod with the preparation of the gospel of peace" (Eph. 6:15). What does "the gospel of peace" refer to (see p. 107)?
7. What resource did the Israelites focus on when confronted with the challenge of removing their enemies from the Promised Land (see pp. 107-8)?
8. When you have a problem in your life, you have to get away from human _____ and stand on God's _____ (see p. 108).
9. What is a recommended formula that will help you to stand strong in God (see p. 110)?
10. What was happening between Euodia and Syntyche, and how was it affecting the Philippian church (see p. 111)?
11. How did Paul present his concern about Euodia and Syntyche to the Philippians (see p. 111)?
12. What kind of people is a truly loving person willing to love (see p. 112)?
13. True love is _____ (see p. 112).
14. What is the nature of Paul's statement in Philippians 4:4 (see p. 113)?
15. What are we to rejoice in (see p. 114)?

16. How frequently should we rejoice? Explain how we can do that (see p. 114).
17. Describe the gentleness Paul showed to the Thessalonians (1 Thess. 2:7; see p. 115).
18. What does the phrase "the Lord is at hand" refer to in Philippians 4:5 (see p. 115)?
19. How can we live a fulfilled life (Phil. 4:8-9; see p. 117)?

Pondering the Principles

1. Standing fast in the Lord means trusting Him completely in every circumstance you encounter. He is our resource, and He can help us handle our problems, even when we don't understand them. Below are some circumstances that Christians sometimes allow themselves to become overwhelmed by as a result of not trusting the Lord. Match up each circumstance with the appropriate verses and memorize that which most speaks to your needs.

   a. Financial worry   a. Romans 8:29-39
   b. Injustice   b. Matthew 28:20b
   c. Doubting your salvation   c. 1 John 1:9
   d. Feeling unforgiven by God   d. Psalm 37:1-11
   e. Loneliness   e. Matthew 6:25-33

2. One element of living a fulfilled life is having a true love for everyone. What are the characteristics of true love according to Matthew 5:43-44, Romans 13:8, and 1 Corinthians 13:4-7? Write them down. Pick out two or three characteristics that you are strong in. If a Christian who was lacking in those areas came up to you and asked how he could develop those characteristics, what would you tell him? Now, pick the two or three characteristics you are weakest in and determine a plan of action you can take to become stronger in those areas.

3. In Philippians 4:4, Paul didn't say you are to rejoice in your circumstances—but in the Lord. Ask yourself: Can God sustain you in the midst of any problem? What good things has the Lord done for you or promised to you that you are thankful for? When you focus on what God has already done for you and all that He has promised to you, then you have much to rejoice

about. When you lose that perspective, you'll stop depending on God and begin depending on your own human resources, which are limited. Develop a habit of constantly remembering God's sustenance and all that He has done for you. With that kind of mind-set, you will be able to rejoice in the Lord always.

Scripture Index

120